Cover painting: *"Sailing Off Gloucester,"* (1880),
by American artist Winslow Homer (1836-1910).
Property of Yale University Art Gallery.

The writer sails alone. He may spend time in his life with
other artists, friends, family, and people he loves, but when
he writes, he is always sailing alone.

Sometimes he has a nautical chart. Sometimes there are
buoys, lighthouses, and channel markers. But for most of
his time, the true writer, consumed by his art, sails in
uncharted waters with no aids to navigation.

The winds and the currents are unpredictable. Reefs are
unmarked. The water depth is unfathomable, so his boat
carries no anchors. At night, the darkness is total. Harbors
are unmarked, appear out of nowhere, so he must decide
quickly whether to finish a trip then, or continue on.

A few on the shore wish him to succeed; a few there wish
him to fail. The great majority of people do not care, and
are totally disinterested in his success or failure.

The writer sails alone.

D1028101

Cover Painting: Winslow Homer
Cover Design: Jamie Korswig Thompson
Printed in the U.S.A.

Sailing Alone
on Sundays

Dan McCullough

Limulus Press®
P.O. Box 2813
Orleans, Massachusetts 02653
LimulusPressInc@aol.com

ISBN: 978-0-9771124-2-5

Cover and book design by Jamie Thompson

Printed in the United States of America

This book is dedicated
to the memory of my father,
who taught me the magic of words,
and whose Celtic seannachie* blood
runs through my veins, and powers
every keystroke of my fingers.

*Seannachie, n. (Gaelic <u>Seanachaidh</u>).
A storyteller among the Highlands of Scotland who
preserved and repeated the traditions of the clans.

(Webster's Revised Unabridged Dictionary, 1913 Edition)

Thanks To _____

The publishers and editors of the *Cape Cod Times*, who have given me the space to express myself at the top of the Op-Ed page every Sunday morning for the past 26 years. Your support has been bountiful, and I am in your debt. More specifically, two men deserve special mention as my editors during my tenure at the Times: my first editor, James Kershner, and my current editor, William Mills.

I must now speak of them: To be successful, every good writer must find his own voice. This is especially true for newspaper columnists, who expose themselves in every column. This voice is the artistic equivalent of a fingerprint or a DNA molecule. It is totally individual; it has its own ways. It regularly breaks rules of style. It isn't always smooth and flowing. It isn't always pretty or comfortable. It has its own quirks and idiosyncrasies. But it's still good writing. Many editors regularly attempt to rein in their writers, to fit them into a pre-determined format of what they – the editors - think should be the writer's style.

Also, not all editors are themselves good writers. But truly gifted editors such as Kershner and Mills are, in fact, good writers themselves. They approach their editing with a writer's eye, with an organic view, seeing the whole piece, not just this adverb, semicolon, or sentence fragment.

These two men have, for the past two and a half decades, watched over my work with a keen eye to making it as good as it can be, without stilling my voice, without compromising my individuality, allowing me to develop that voice, to express myself in my terms. We have not always agreed, but they have encouraged me when appropriate, and made suggestions for change when appropriate, always treating me and my work with the greatest of respect and dignity.

Thanks, guys. You have made me better, and I am in your debt.

Thanks Also To

My faithful readers, hundreds of whom have been with me for decades. You send e-mails and stamped mails; you call me on the phone; you stop and say hello in restaurants, in airports; you send messages via students, and you shout at me at traffic lights. And finally, heartfelt thanks to those of you who have consistently encouraged - sometimes harassed - me publicly and privately – to put a collection of my columns into print.

In this connection, three individuals deserve special mention for consistently reminding me that I need to write this volume you hold in your hands. These are Rich Eldred, long-time sports writer for the *Cape Codder* newspaper, who has hectored me for years to write this book. Also thanks to my dear friend John Crane for his decades of support of all my writing: newspaper columns and short stories. John is a career newspaperman, and is today still an actively employed writer, so he knows writing. Also thanks to my buddy and faithful reader, housewright Jack Goff who, for years has read my stuff and reported to me on its substance. Although not a writer, he is a voracious reader and when it comes to my writing, he "gets it."

Special thanks to Jamie Thompson for her tireless work on the total and detailed design of every page of this book. Thanks also to her colleagues at Thompson's Printing: Matt, Joann and Roz who also made this project easier on me.

Thanks to my beloved Annie Wood for her many continuous years of support and encouragement in all the projects of my life.

And finally, thanks to my friend Lewis who taught me that, in the end, all that mattered was that you loved and were loveable. (Lewis has no last name – cats don't have last names).

Foreword _____

All writings contained herein were originally published in the *Cape Cod Times* between 1987 and 2013. With the exception of occasional and very minor editing changes, they are substantially intact in their original form. I have done this deliberately to maintain the character and atmosphere of the times and occasions in which they were written over these 26 years.

A special note to the reader: this is not a "Greatest Hits" album, nor is it a collection of "The Best Of..." I have selected the pieces for this collection in an attempt to provide the reader with a sampling of the diverse topics that my 1400 consecutive Sunday columns represent. Thank you for that opportunity. I hope I have been successful. Only you can be the judge of that.

Enjoy...

Dan McCullough

Rock Harbor
Orleans, Massachusetts
August 19th, 2013

Table of Contents

_____ The Children

THE WINTER OF JESSE BARR

This is the first column I ever wrote for the Cape Cod Times. The Orleans bureau chief for the paper had read some of my work and one day, in the spring of 1987, he suggested I should send some of my stuff in to the newspaper. I submitted this piece and they published it. One thousand, three hundred consecutive Sundays later, I'm still at it. The last two words of this column are still true to me.

I'm not sure exactly what got me thinking about Jesse Barr today. I was out hauling my lobster pots, thinking about how my close friend, Bruce Macfarlane, had helped me get them rigged out this spring. He said that he would help me, but when I went to pick them up, they were completely rigged and ready to go, saving me time and headaches. He didn't say anything - just gave them to me as they were. He knew I was busy and needed help, that was all the prodding he needed. That's Bruce.

As I hauled in the first pot (full of crabs), I got to thinking about how a bunch of other friends had helped me roof my house in Brewster a few years ago, when I was even shorter of cash than I am now. One spring morning, thirteen of them showed up with pickup trucks, ladders, tools and enthusiasm, and we shingled one of those old sea captains' houses over on 6A in one day.

As I set out for the next pot, I reflected how another group of us had helped a friend build his new house. Husbands, wives, children, in-laws, neighbors, friends and dogs showed up at the building site for a few months until the job was done. It felt good; we had a sense of extended family, togetherness, something like that. It was hard to define.

Anyway, by the time I hauled and set my last pot, turned into the southwest wind and headed for home, I was thinking about Cape Cod people, a sense of community spirit and - Jesse Barr.

I never met Jesse Barr. Most people who knew of him never met him, either. He was a five-year-old boy who lived and died in Orleans. He had cancer. He had a very difficult case of cancer, and spent the most of his five years fighting the disease which finally took him a little over a year ago. But my thoughts today were not about the courage and fight that the little guy showed in his battle, but were about us - the people whose lives he came into in the winter of 1985-86.

When the medical bills for this little gladiator became astronomical, beyond the capacity of even a wealthy family, which the Barrs are not, I think it was the Lower Cape CB'ers Association that started a fund to help defray these expenses. What happened next was electric. The number of people and organizations involved increased logarithmically.

Special events blossomed all over the lower Cape. There were mayonnaise jars with Jesse Barr's picture on them at Cumberland Farms, Stop & Shop, and up at Fuller's Package Store as well as in every other convenience store, supermarket, and liquor store in the area. Laundromats and post offices were emblazoned with posters and flyers telling of band concerts, car washes, a long distance race. Restaurants and bars all had jars or baskets with "Jesse Barr" tacked on the outside. At the Land-Ho! it became a routine for some of the locals to decline the "one for the road" and stuff the money for the last drink in the jar. The Barley Neck Inn in Orleans hosted an evening of local entertainment; the Orleans Methodist Church declared March of 1986 "Jesse Barr Month" and took up special collections on Sundays. Schoolchildren saved pennies. It was incredible. It was wildfire. It was like a nuclear reaction.

By mid-May, over $70,000 had been raised and a community had been changed. We had been brought together in spirit and enthusiasm. The winter had been the shortest in recent memory. We felt like the whole winter had been one big family reunion. We felt as if we had done this all before; we must have, how else could one explain how easily it came to us? It seemed so natural and easy.

Jesse Barr died in late May of that year, and it was sad. Not as sad as one might think, however. The enthusiasm of the winter carried through the funeral and burial and life went on. But we were changed. We looked at each other differently, at least for a little while.

Priests, ministers, rabbis, teachers and others spend most of their lives trying to bring out the good in us. They try to help us to be the best that we can be - unselfish, caring, sympathetic, sensitive, aware of the needs of others, etc. This five-year-old boy came into our world, and in the last few months of his short life touched more of us than most sermons, TV shows, or inspirational speeches could.

So I guess that's how I got to thinking about Jesse Barr today. I have a feeling I'll think of him whenever I think of the power of goodness within each of us, and how easy it is to tap that goodness and come together to help each other when we have the will to do so.

Thanks, Jesse.

REFLECTIONS ON A FRIEND'S LOSS

I think that only another parent can understand what it would be like to lose a child. In this 1990 column, I reflect upon this.

I got home late from a long day's work this past week. I was hungry and tired. As I walked in the door, I pulled my sweatshirt over my head and let it slip to the floor. I dropped my briefcase, newspapers and mail in the chair by my desk, and went across to the kitchen to check out the possible menu for the evening meal.

The refrigerator didn't promise much: some frozen chili, frozen chicken soup, some bread, cheese, skim milk, a bag of Maine potatoes and a half stick of pepperoni. I decided that it would take more culinary imagination than I possessed to make those ingredients into a coherent meal.

Reluctantly, I put my sweatshirt back on and headed for the market. I needed something quick, simple and easy. A minute later I was in the parking lot of the big Stop & Shop in Orleans. I grabbed my little list and my checkbook from the dashboard of the truck and headed in to the store.

I was scratching items off the list pretty quickly, and was just about done when I came to the end of an aisle and just about collided with my old friend, Bob Porter. Bob is a psychologist. He's good at what he does. He was state director of mental health for the Cape and Islands for a while. Now I think he does mostly private practice and consulting. I've known some of his clients over the years. This past winter, one of them told me straight out that Bob had saved his life. I've heard other similar second-hand stories about his professional skills.

Porter and I used to spend a lot more time together than we do now. He got married just about the time that I got unmarried, and I think that was part of it. But we've been friends for close to twenty years. Regretfully, nowadays our conversations now are restricted to serendipitous meetings in the lobby of the Brewster Post Office, outside a shop in the Cape Cod Mall, or perhaps at a conference at the Community College.

Bob is a wiry, tightly-wrapped guy. He's trim and fit looking; he was an iron worker when he was younger, before he found his career. I'll bet he doesn't weigh ten pounds more today than when he was twenty-one. I'm always happy to see him. Like me, he's a physically affectionate guy, and doesn't mind giving another guy a hug in public. I lined my shopping carriage up beside him and wrapped my arms around him.

Bob is the father of two sons, Steve and Gary. Both his boys were born years before my son, but I watched the two of them grow into teen age as my little one was a middle school child. The older of the two, Steve, was a special kid. Musically talented, intelligent, imaginative, and friendly, he made it a treat to run into him anywhere. I can picture his face now, a face much like his father's, with the same sparkling eyes and open smile.

When Steve was in his early twenties, about ten years ago, he went to Europe. I think his presence there was musically oriented. He was with a band and they were on tour, or he was there to study music, something like that. He and his friends were taking a train through France one day.

The message which came to Bob Porter from Europe that day changed his life. There had been a train crash, a bad one. People were killed. Steve was one of those people. He was dead. Sorry.

I remember the day I heard the news. I was with my son.

We were riding around, running errands. I made a note to myself to call Bob as soon as we got home. As we pulled into the driveway, I looked at the little kid next to me on the front seat of my truck. I thought about Steve Porter, dead in France. I thought about my friend, Bob. I thought about my son, and I thought about myself.

I got into the house and went for the phone in the kitchen. No, no, this wouldn't do, I said to myself. I'd use the phone in my office upstairs. I sat at my desk and dialed the number. Before it could ring on the other end, in Bob's house, I hung up. This was no time for a faceless telephone conversation, I decided. I'd talk to him in person. Yeah, that was the best way to do this. A few weeks passed. By that time I decided that I would write to him. I'm best at expressing myself in writing, much better than in person. That would be the best way to do it, for sure.

I sat down to write several times and was unable to tell my friend how I felt. That's not exactly true; I think I was able to tell him how I felt, but I figured that it wouldn't mean much to him since how I was feeling had more to do with me and my son than it did with him and his dead son. The words seemed stupid, inappropriate and selfish. After awhile, I stopped trying to write. And I never made the phone call.

The next time I ran into Bob, Steve's name was not mentioned. As the years went by, and Bob and I spent time with each other, I never mentioned Steve.

Ever.

As we stood by the canned goods in the market this week and talked of many things, Steve's name popped out of my mouth. It was an accident. We were talking, I think, about the passage of time, and I started a sentence by saying something like, "When Steve and Gary were little boys...."

I couldn't believe I had actually mentioned him. Bob didn't

even notice. We continued our talk, and soon, by mutually obvious body language and the tempo of the conversation, it was time to go. We made some tentative plans to communicate by telephone. Bob wrote something on the back of one of his professional cards, and we turned away from one another.

I watched him start to move away.

I said his name, quietly.

He turned back, just a few feet away, and looked at me.

I told him that I had never mentioned Steve all those years because it was too painful for me to do so. I told him that all I could think of when I thought of Steve was my own son. Dammit, I said to him, they even look alike, tall, dark-haired with handsome smiles.

I told him that I felt like a survivor after Steve had been killed. I felt uncomfortable even thinking about him. I told him that I couldn't even write about it, no matter how I tried. I watched his eyes fill up as I spoke. His face was getting a little blurry from my perspective, as well too. We wordlessly embraced, and then he was gone.

A few minutes later, as I walked across my yard, I stopped and listened. Sometimes, from where I live, it's hard to tell if the noise in the air is the wind or the pounding Atlantic surf on the shore. Sometimes you have to listen for a second to tell the difference.

I didn't have listen very carefully tonight. The difference was clear to me. A lot of things were more clear to me.

THINGS THAT CANNOT BE FIXED

This column, published in 2009, addresses the universal experience each of us has when we – sometimes quickly, sometimes slowly – come to a realization that there are some things that will never be made right again.

I remember leaning over my father's dead body, and gently placing my lips against his forehead. He had been dead for not very long; his body was not cold.

I also remember later that day the long drive back from Worcester to Cape Cod, alone in my truck. It was a Monday, Presidents' Day, in the middle of February. I had been away in China over the winter break between semesters at the college, and had not seen my parents for a couple of months. On impulse, I decided to take a ride up to visit them just for the day.

My father had died within minutes of my arrival, a totally unexpected event. He hadn't been in seriously ill health, or at least not in worse health than most people in their mid-80s.

I didn't take any time off from school. I had lectures scheduled the next day, so I got a good night's sleep and in the morning I drove over to the college and taught my courses as if nothing unusual had happened in my life. I didn't even mention it to my students.

I believed that's what my father would have done, and I knew for sure that's what he would have wanted me to do.

When I gave my father a goodbye kiss that day, I remember that there were no tears running down my face. And I can remember thinking that what it meant to be a mature and healthy adult – having the ability to understand and accept what was happening in front of you and to deal with the cards that had been dealt you that day.

"My father is dead," I was thinking as I stood there – "And there is nothing I can do about it."

I'd like to think that the kind of wisdom that allows us to accept the things we cannot change was something that I learned from my father, but I don't believe that to be true. I loved the old man dearly; he was my hero. Almost all the things I love about myself these days I learned from my father. But not all. I do believe there are things that cannot be taught.

I believe that Aeschylus, the Greek thinker who lived around the time of Socrates, had it right when, he described the gaining of wisdom: True wisdom cannot be taught to us; We need to suffer its lessons in the fire of its forge before we can attain it.

And the coming of wisdom is not something that we wake up some morning and find that we have. It falls, as Aeschylus said, "Drop by drop upon the heart," and we possess it long before we are aware that we do.

And then days come to us when we are standing by a car with a flat tire out on a highway in a mountain pass in Colorado, and we realize that we are going to miss our flight from Denver to Beijing. Or we realize that we have thrown our only copy of three years of Ph.D. research into an incinerator at the Lexington Town Dump, and left the other bag with the week's used newspapers on the front seat of the car. Or when we stand by a parent's dead body.

And it is then that we realize that we have actually attained some kind of wisdom, and we have no idea when it arrived, where it came from, or when it started.

I reflected upon this last consideration – when it starts – in a conversation I had a few days ago with a woman close to me. She and her husband have a four-year-old boy, and like his parents, the little boy is an emotionally sensitive person.

I hadn't seen her or her family in a while, and she called this past Thursday to catch up on what was going on in our lives. We talked about my family and the comings and goings over the holidays, and then I asked about her family as well.

"We had a little trauma while taking down the Christmas tree the other day," she told me. She went on to explain.

She and the little four-year-old were dismantling the Christmas tree and taking down the lights from the windows. He has a special Christmas tree ornament that he loves more than any other. His mother described it as a beautiful crystal globe with a Christmas Tree on the inside of the globe. "Very special," she repeated.

Anyway, they wanted to give this ornament special treatment, and she sent him out to the other room to put it in a special box until next year. The shiny hardwood floors in the house didn't provide much friction between their surface and the little boy's morning socks he was wearing. He slipped and fell, and with him went the little ornament, sailing through the air to shatter into hundreds of tiny pieces on the floor.

His mother told me he was inconsolable. "I want you to fix it!" he kept saying through his tears. "Can't we fix it?"

I could picture a little boy sitting on the floor with shattered pieces of crystal glass spread out around him and listening to his mother's words telling him, "It can't be fixed."

Ah, those words, "It can't be fixed." How our acceptance of them is so often the beginning of wisdom, even in the middle of such great pain.

Like I've said, I don't know when this wisdom begins, but I think it might begin when we are teary-eyed little children looking up at our mother as she utters those horrible words:

"It can't be fixed."

TRAVELLING WITH HER OWN ANGEL

Many people have no idea how much teachers love their students. In this 2003 piece, I tried to show how much.

My friend Carol says that she is not a particularly religious person. She is a good and decent human being, trustworthy and faithful, with a high sense of moral behavior and social responsibility, but not, as she herself says, a religious person.

That's why she's always wondered about that little guardian angel on the lapel of one of her favorite jackets. The jacket is from the Hard Rock Café in Los Angeles. When she graduated from college, her sister Linda, as a graduation gift, took her to Hollywood for a girls' tour to the West Coast, and bought her the jacket there. When she got back to Cape Cod, she took the pin from her jewel box and secured it to the collar of the denim jacket from L.A. It's been there for a dozen years, maybe longer. "I had the little guardian angel pin for a long time," she says when asked. "I think a friend gave it to me maybe 15 years ago. I'm not sure why I wear it."

She makes her living doing one of the most important jobs on earth – I mean this literally – one of the most important jobs on the planet earth. She is a kindergarten teacher - here on Cape Cod. I've seen her on her way to school in the morning, all brushed and combed with a fresh dress and sensible shoes on – ready to take on 50 five-year-olds for the day. And I've seen her at the end of the day, as well, looking as though she'd been mugged by a bunch of urban punks, her hair pulled back together haphazardly, her dress wrinkled and askew, one of her earrings missing, with remnants of paint still on her fingernails.

But she loves her job. Before the end of the first week of school, she knows each of her students by name, and by the end of the second week, she has fallen in love with each of them, no exception. And since many of them stay in the same school building as they move from her kindergarten to the first, second, and third grades, she continues to stay in touch with them, seeing them in the hallways, cafeteria and library for years to come. And, of course, like any teacher, she has those students that she especially remembers after they leave her care. The reasons why she might remember one student or another would be as diverse as the students. One might have a special sense of humor; another might be the class clown; another might be an exceptionally bright or exceptionally difficult student.

When asked what she remembers about third-grader Katelynn Bearse, Carol instantly brightens up. "Spunk," she says. "She was just a spunky little kindergartner. Plenty of chutzpah," she says with a smile. "I just loved her." When Katelynn finished kindergarten, she went to the next grades in the same building, so the two of them kept in touch. "She was definitely one of my favorites," Carol says.

Katelynn was born with serious cardiac problems. She had surgery after surgery from infancy right up until this year. This spring, her family took her to Children's Hospital in Boston for more surgery to fix a problem with one of the valves in her heart. Someone had told Carol that the surgery was a success, that one of the other valves in her heart had almost spontaneously started to function once the first valve had been fixed. "It was wonderful. She seemed like her old self," Carol said this week. "I saw her at school, gave her a hug and told her I'd never seen her with so much energy."

But apparently things were not as well as they seemed. An infection, or some other medical problem arose about a month ago, and Katelynn was back in the hospital. Things did not go well.

If you read this newspaper regularly, especially if you read it this past Wednesday, June 11, you would have seen something amazing, something very unusual. You would have seen the smiling face of a nine-year-old girl beaming out from the most unlikely place in the newspaper to find such a smiling face. You would have seen the smiling face of Katelynn Bearse, spunky and courageous, looking out at you from the top right-hand corner of the obituary page.

Around her are the stories of other Cape Codders, stories of people who lived into their eighth or ninth decades of life. And there, among them, a little girl who never made it to one decade.

It's customary, as you may know, to print a few lines in bold type after a person's name at the top of an obituary. "President of Baxter College," or "Founded Harris Lumber Company," or "Curator of Reptiles in Sweden," are typical of the summaries one might find at the top of various newspaper obits.

At the top of Katelynn's obituary, it said that she enjoyed dancing and singing. What a wonderful way to be remembered. Forget all the other worldly achievements, degrees and honors one might attain in a lifetime, however long that life might have been. How beautiful to be remembered as someone who "Enjoyed dancing, singing."

So, a week ago today, Katelynn's brave little heart gave out, and her spirit and her spunk went with her to another place, where there will be no more surgeries, no more pain. This past week, Carol and her classroom volunteer, Lucy, left the school building after classes and headed for the funeral home over on Station Avenue in South Yarmouth, not far from the elementary school. The day had been a beautiful and sunny day, reminiscent of the majesty of Tuesday, but by the time the two women parked their car at the funeral home, it had begun to get dark and threatening. The radio said it was already raining in Boston.

Inside the building, there was little laughter or joy. When an old man dies, his cronies can stand out on the steps, smoking cigarettes and laughing at stories of the old days, and joking about the deceased. But when a nine-year-old girl dies, there are no stories about the good old days, no stories about her history. There were no smiles or laughter in that room, just the quiet sounds of shoes moving across carpeted floors, of people exchanging muted sentiments as they hugged each other, pressing tears into each other's shoulders.

As Carol knelt by the casket and looked down at the beautiful face of her student, she realized she had her favorite jacket on – the one with the angel on the lapel. She checked with Katelynn's mother, and, with her approval, she unpinned the angel from her jacket, reached over and pinned it on Katelynn's dress....

... saying goodbye to a courageous little girl off on a journey. Her own angel traveling with her.

TWO WORDS TO THE MAN IN RED

Sometimes a word from a child (or in this 1993 column – two words) can change a man's whole day.

This past Thursday, as you may recall, was a dismal affair, a December kind of a day. In the morning, the weather report reaffirmed what my sailor's eye already knew: "Winter storm warnings....winds 45 mph....up to 60 mph....possibility of heavy rain....heavy snow....beach erosion....northeast winds...." etc.

After the weather report, my day continued pretty much in the same vein. By 8:30 in the morning, I was sitting in a doctor's office on Lewis Bay Road in Hyannis. He was sticking needles into me, and alternately cutting on my body with scalpels and razors.

By 9:30, I was at work. I returned four phone calls (two no-answers, one busy, one message machine). My next stop was at the copy center. I needed to run off a seven-page article from a journal for the students in my Introduction to Philosophy course. Seven original pages x twenty-five students = 175 pages of copy. No problem. Ten, maybe fifteen minutes, max. But things weren't going well at the Xerox machine this morning. The machine would print one page, then a red- lighted message would come on, saying, "PLEASE WAIT". After a aggravating space of several seconds, the message would go off, and the machine would print one more page, then the message again, and so on.

Fortunately, Dick Northrop, the professional who runs the copy center, was standing just a few feet away, working on the big grandmother of all copying machines.

"Hey Dick," I say.

"Yeah?" Dick answers, slowly coming over to the machine I'm on.

"You ever see anything like this?" I ask, pointing down to the courteous (PLEASE WAIT) but stuttering machine. Dick stands there next to me. We watch the machine print beautiful copies, one every eight or nine seconds.

"No, I never have," he says, shaking his head.

"Uh....me neither," I mutter, still staring down at the machine. We both stand there for a minute, staring at the machine, then he returns to his work. I wait; the machine prints. I wait; the machine prints. It takes me half an hour to print a 4-minute job.

By noon, I'm planning a Saturday morning ten-mile hike around Great Island in Wellfleet with the Explorers' Club at the college. Fifteen or twenty students are sitting on the floor outside my office. The weather is a key topic of conversation. I'm not happy about the whole thing. I want the weather to be either good - so we can plan the trip, or bad - so we can cancel. This in-between stuff is not what I want on my plate today.

Halfway through the meeting, the local anesthetic from this morning's encounter with the surgical knife has worn off. A little later, on the way to class, the weather begins to come in, as predicted. This is not a good day.

Driving home in the storm at 5:30, I realize I need some stuff for dinner. I stay on the highway to the Eastham rotary and head for the big Stop & Shop in Orleans. As I cross the darkened parking lot, the sleet stings my face, turning my cheeks the color of the red bandana wrapped around my head, and the bright red "OHIO STATE" hooded sweatshirt. Once inside the door of the brightly-lit store, I brush the little pieces of ice out of my giant white beard, snatch up a hand-basket, and head down an aisle.

I'm absentmindedly staring at 300 different kinds of bread on a shelf when I hear something behind me. It's a voice. A small voice. I process the three syllables in the two words just spoken to me as I turn around and look into the face of a little boy, three, maybe four years old. He's sitting in a big shopping cart. His mother is behind him, her back to us, picking out some stuff from the frozen food section.

I can't believe what I've just heard from this kid's mouth. He's just sitting there looking at me. He's not nervous, he's not excited. He's just looking up at me with a wide-eyed open trusting look one might have for an old friend. It's a private moment between me and this young citizen.

This isn't the way this day was supposed to end, I'm thinking. He must see I'm a little stunned, so he calmly repeats the words.

"Hi, Santa."

Still stunned, I somehow regain my composure, and manage a big throaty, "Ho-ho-Ho!" I ask him if he's been a good boy. He wordlessly nods his head matter-of-factly, as if to say, "Of course, you idiot. You think I'd be saying 'hello' to you if I hadn't been the best little boy in the whole world?"

By this time, the mother has turned around; I catch her eye. She's coming in on the end of the conversation. One look at me and she knows all is well. Then it's over. I'm down the aisle one way, they the other.

I'm alone in the store, but I'm wishing I weren't because I can't get this damned smile off my face. I must look like an idiot. Remember when you were a kid in school and something funny happened and you wanted to laugh, but you couldn't because you'd get in trouble? Remember what kid's faces looked like who were trying not to smile? Well that's what I looked like.

I get to the check-out, still in the same condition. The

woman at the register has concluded I've been smoking something funny. I can tell by her face, looking at my face, trying not to laugh.

Eight hours later, it's after 2 A.M. I'm home alone working. The wind is howling outside. The sleet is tattooing the window next to my desk. The kid's face comes back to me. I shake my head, still smiling.

Funny, but as I look back on the previous day, the 23 seconds with that kid is all I really remember.

CHILDREN DIGGING IN THE GROUND

My father had always told me about his working at a young age, but until my son was that age, I don't think it really hit me. This 2013 column reflects upon that.

My father would have been 107 years old if he had lived until last week. But he's been dead for 20 years or so, so I was startled to see him in a photograph in the New York Times last week. The article was a February 26th front-page piece on the use of child labor in the coal mines of India. At the top of the front page is a photo of a young boy, a head-shot of just his face, his skin and hair darkened with coal dust as he stares into the camera.

The text of the article continued onto Page 11. That's where I saw my old man. It's a large photo – almost half the page. Taken deep in a coal mine in India, the photo appears at first glance to be in black and white, but as the reader's eyes move around the photograph, there are a few streaks of color. But it's a black and white picture.

In the photo there are three boys. One, in the right-hand side of the frame seems to be turning toward the camera as he is exiting the picture, shovel in hand. On the extreme left-hand side of the picture, another boy is exiting the photo, also with shovel in hand. His body is partially cropped out of the photograph; only his left arm and leg are visible – his face is not in the picture. Along the left-hand side of the photograph a sturdy bamboo ladder, blackened with coal dust and black mud, rises out of the black chamber upward, at a very steep angle. It seems to be moving toward a light source above.

In the middle of the picture is the third boy, sitting under the ladder and the light, some pages in his hand, reading. The caption explains that he is studying English on his work break. It's hard to tell how old these boys are. The text of the article tells of young teenagers working in the mines, as well as reports of some children as young as five. It was when I looked at that boy and read what he was doing that I saw my father.

But I'm getting a little ahead of myself here. I'll come back to the 2013 coal mines of India in a couple of minutes.

One day many years ago, back in the mid-1970s, my parents had driven to Cape Cod on a beautiful warm fall day in the end of October for my son's eighth birthday party. There were drinks and cake, games and presents strewn around the table in the big kitchen of the house in Brewster. There were eight-year-old boys running in and out the back door, the constant slamming of the screen door was almost drowned out by the screaming and laughing as they bobbed for apples in a big wash bucket outside on the deck. I had slipped coins of various denominations into each apple, and I was the adult towel-master as each dripping little boy came up from underwater, with or without an apple in his teeth.

After the apple-bobbing was over and the boys had moved on to some kind of a ball game in the yard, I was dripping wet from all the splashing. I wrapped a big towel around my neck and went back into the kitchen where some adults, my parents included, were sitting at the table. As I passed my father, I gave him a wet hug and then dropped into a chair opposite him. Our eyes met and we just nodded wordlessly to each other, a habit we had fallen into sometime after I had reached adulthood.

Minutes later, my son came running into the kitchen and

stopped at his grandfather's side to give him a hug. My father made some exclamation about how fast the boy had become eight years old. Then he looked down at my son and said in a matter-of-fact voice, "When I was eight, my brother Alec and I were working at the coal mines in Pennsylvania. They used to come and pick us up at the orphanage in a big black bus." My son glanced lovingly up at his grandfather and nodded as if that were the most natural thing in the world.

I looked at the two Daniels in my life: one eight years old – the other 70 years old, and I tried to picture my father at age eight, waiting at the side of the road outside a Pennsylvania orphanage, waiting with the other little boys for the big black bus to take them to the coal mine. What was he feeling as stood there? What did he think of what was happening to him? What did he think was his future? I looked at my son in his grandfather's arms, just a baby really, a third-grader at the Brewster Elementary School. I looked at the cake, the sounds of his friends outside, the brightly-colored wrapping paper discarded around the kitchen, and I understood then that my father had known none of this. None. Overcome with emotion, I stood and went out the door into the yard, alone in my thoughts.

There was no education at the orphanage. My father did not learn to read until he was almost ten years old, after he had left the orphanage and went to live on a farm where two of his older sisters were governesses to the farm family children. But once he learned to read, it became one of his life's passions. When I picture my father today, I picture him reading.

So when I held the New York Times article in my hands last week, and looked at the young boy in the coal mine, sitting under the ladder on his work break, learning to read English, I knew in my mind that I was looking at a kid in India. But

NAKED BOY'S REWARD: A GUINEA PIG

My young five-year-old grandson called me on the phone the other day. "Papa," he said. "I saved the day!" Then he handed the phone to his father, who told me the whole story, published in 2010.

Five-year old Alexander McCullough, my grandson, has been pestering his parents for a pet guinea pig. The non-existent pet actually has a name. If he ever had a guinea pig, Alexander says, he would name it "Sunflower," an animal that exists only in Alexander's imagination.

There are 10 National Seashores in the United States. The easternmost is our own Cape Cod National Seashore, and the westernmost is Point Reyes National Seashore on the San Andreas Fault, north of San Francisco. For a kid raised on the sands of Cape Cod National Seashore, it seems only natural that my son would wind up visiting the western seashore if he were ever in the area...as he was last week.

He flew out of Logan Airport to San Francisco for a medical conference. As the conference was winding down, Kim, my daughter-in-law, and my two grandsons, Alexander, and his one-year-old baby brother, Andrew, flew out to join him for an April mini-vacation among the giant firs and redwoods of Northern California, and a tour of the Point Reyes National Seashore.

They rent a little cottage on a creek there for a few days. The cottage is affiliated with a large hotel, but is several hundred feet down the road, not visible from the hotel, so they have total privacy. It's a cozy cottage; there's a large hot tub on the back deck, a fireplace, a little kitchen, comfortable beds – you get the picture.

On the second day they are there, my son gets up early. There's a chill in the air. The temperatures in the woods of Northern California in April are comparable to what they are here on Cape Cod. He lights a fire in the fireplace to warm up the place, and then notices the hot tub outside, so he turns that on as well.

Sleepy-eyed 5-year-old Alexander, joins him for his good morning snuggle. They hatch a plan, and soon they have stripped all their clothes off, are stepping naked out onto the deck, quickly slipping out of the cool morning air into the steaming waters of the tub.

Minutes later, Kim and one-year-old toddler Andrew appear in the doorway to the deck, smiling at the would-be Californians soaking naked in the hot tub surrounded by the giant forest. Kim looks around to double-check the privacy of the area, strips herself, and then Andrew, naked, replacing his clothes with a little swim diaper, and soon all four family members are <u>au naturel</u>, the only article of clothing outside the cottage walls is Andrew's tiny swim diaper.

My son notices that the cottage door is not quite closed, and, aware of conserving the fireplace heat inside, gets up, slams the door tightly shut, then rejoins his naked family in the tub.

They splash around, laughing and playing in a pre-breakfast visit. Alexander can swim, so he loves the water, and baby Andrew gets put in and out of the tub regularly, as babies that young should not stay in hot tubs for long periods. In and out is OK. He probably thinks it's a game.

Well, after a half hour or so, it's time to get dried off and dressed for another California day. Going for some nice warm towels, my son gets up and crosses the deck to the door that he had slammed tightly shut half an hour ago.

Right. It's locked.

In the chilly morning air, the wet and naked family frantically circumambulates the house looking for an unlocked door or window.

Nothing. This cabin might as well be a bank on a Sunday.

My son finds a door on the other side of the house that has two inside locks on it: one at the top of the door, the other down near the bottom. He gets the bottom lock loosened, but that only tightens the top one. The bottom of the door is opened only three or four inches, just wide enough for a man's fist. Seeing no other alternatives, my son declares that he'll just have to kick the door open, causing hundreds of dollars of damage.

A little voice begins to speak next to him. He looks down into Alexander's eyes as he says: "If I had a guinea pig, we could slide him in through the opening, and he could go across the room, get the key and bring it back to us."

The silence following Alexander's observation is broken by his mother's voice: "Alexander, if you put on Andrew's swim diaper, go up to the hotel and get a spare key from the manager, I'll get you a guinea pig."

"Really?" the little voice says.

"I'm a woman of my word," she replies seriously.

Alexander thinks for second. "I'll do it," he says. Kim wrings out the clean diaper and fastens it to Alexander's body. It's a diaper for a one-year-old. Even on his child's body, it looks tiny, like a five-year-old in a white bikini on the French Riviera.

Totally naked and barefoot father and bikinied and barefoot son walk out to the road leading up to the hotel. They rehearse Alexander's soliloquy at the hotel; "I need the key to the Creekside Cottage."

"You got it?" father says. "I got it," son replies, and as

naked father watches from behind a giant Douglas Fir tree, the little white diaper wobbles its way down the road, turns up the lawn to the hotel, crosses a patio, opens a door, and steps into a large dining room filled with breakfasting hotel guests.

A strange sight: a preschooler in a diaper coming out of the early morning woods into a crowded hotel dining room. But minutes later, Alexander is back at the cottage hot tub and is handing the key to his father. As my son reaches up to take the key, Alexander holds on to the key for a second, and says something to the effect of: "We spoke earlier about a guinea pig?"

The family arrived back in Boston late Saturday night. After church on Sunday morning, the four of them go to a pet store on the North Shore. I talk to my son day or two later.

"Well," he says, "There's a new family member here at the house."

"Name?" I ask.

"Sunflower," he says.

The Heart

THE JOHNNY CASH STORY

This 1989 piece tells about going to a Johnny Cash concert in Boston Garden. It went national shortly after I wrote it, was published in at least one hardcover book, and I was told that it now hangs in the Country and Western Hall of Fame in Nashville, Tennessee. It's definitely one of my favorites.

As I pulled my truck into a parking place in West Barnstable this week, a song which I hadn't heard for years came on the radio. It was, "Ring of Fire," a classic hit by the famous country and western singer, Johnny Cash.

By the time I had backed into the parking place, the song was only half over, so I just sat there with the truck running and the radio playing, and listened to the rest of the song. I was already five minutes late for a meeting, but the song had me by the throat. When the song ended, I shut off the truck, grabbed my books and stuff, and headed across the parking lot. I wasn't much watching where I was going that morning; the song had taken me back to my first (and last) Johnny Cash concert. It was at Boston Garden a few years ago.

Now, let's get one thing straight right from the start: I am not now, nor have I ever been, a REAL big fan of country and western music. As a kind of spoof on country music, Steve Goodman, the Chicago songwriter, once developed a formula for the perfect country and western song. I don't remember the rules exactly, but to write the perfect song, one had to include: mama, trains, gettin' drunk, a motel, a pickup truck, a dog, jail, divorce, and a long-distance phone call.

I like that; I like it a lot. It probably tells you how seriously I take country music. One of my favorites is, "The Night I Talked to Jesus On My CB Radio" (a real song, honest!). And another (for football fans): "Dropkick me Jesus Through the Goal Posts of Life."

So anyway, back to Johnny Cash:

My friend, Bobby, is a Down's Syndrome adult. You know, what we used to call "mentally retarded." His best friend, Gordon, is a congenitally brain-damaged adult. At the time this story takes place, both these guys are in their late teens. Now I've know both these guys since they were babies. I'm Bobby's godfather, and Gordon's mother is a woman from my old neighborhood. I played ball with her brothers (Gordon's uncles) and we went to school together.

Bobby and Gordon grew up together and they were inseparable. What a picture they made together. Gordon was a black kid, over six feet tall, with long black fingers, long black arms and legs, and beautiful big brown eyes, which were only magnified by the glasses he wore because he was visually handicapped. Gordon was so skinny, he could hide behind a telephone pole, and often did, teasing Bobby. His six-foot-plus frame could not have weighed 120 pounds. I could (and often did) pick him up with one hand.

Bobby, on the other hand, had Irish white skin, blue eyes, also magnified by the glass frames of his handicap, and was built like a professional wrestler. He was about five foot, six inches tall, round-shouldered and strong as a little bull. He would often pick Gordon up in jest, much to Gordon's displeasure. What a visual duet the two of them presented, walking down the street together or sitting on Bobby's front porch steps together, talking things over. They went to separate schools but spent every free waking hour together. They were two of the most free spirits I've ever known. I didn't know anyone who knew them who didn't love them. They sure loved each other.

Oh, yeah, Johnny Cash.

Well anyway, the one thing these two characters had in common was a passionate addiction for the music of Johnny

Cash. They had Johnny Cash posters in their rooms, Johnny Cash albums and cassettes, Johnny Cash T-shirts, picture books, magazine articles, memorabilia, ad infinitum.

So one day, I read in the newspaper that Johnny Cash is going to be at Boston Garden. I think for a minute, maybe less, say to myself, "What the hell," and head up to Boston Garden. The guy behind the ticket window says, "How many tickets?" I tell him three. "Where do you want to sit?" he says. I tell him money is no object; I want the three best seats in the house. I explain to the guy that the tickets are for a couple special needs guys who love Johnny Cash.

"Oh, really?" the guy says. "My granddaughter is Down Syndrome...she's the love of my life."

"Hmm, let me see," he says as he scans the little pigeonholes on the wall next to him, looking for the three best seats in the house. As you might guess, he found them: first row center.

Now I don't know where this next idea came from, but on the way home, I started to wonder what the possibilities might be of Bobby and Gordon getting a chance to maybe get Cash's autograph, or something. But I don't know any Boston promoters or wheeler-dealers. I'm just a guy whose has two special friends who would give anything have Cash's autograph, or maybe (Oh God! Could it possibly happen?) shake his hand. Minutes later, I'm on the phone with Ernie Santasuosso, entertainment columnist at the Boston Globe. He had reviewed a rock concert earlier in the week, so I dialed the Globe and asked for him. He picked up the phone.

The conversation began, "Hi, Ernie, you don't know me; we've never met, and I don't have any friends in the entertainment business, but I've got these two kids, special kids, friends of mine....." and I tell him my story. A few minutes later, Santasuosso says, "Give me your number; I'll see what I can do, and get back to you." (Sure, I think, he'll get back to me, all right).

Twenty minutes later, the phone rings. It's Santasuosso. "Call this number at the Sonesta Hotel in Cambridge," he says. "Ask for Fred Taylor; he's expecting your call. I just talked to him. He's at the hotel with Cash." (With Cash? With JOHNNY Cash? This guy's at the hotel with JOHNNY CASH?....Hey, wait a minute, this is getting a little too close!) Five minutes later, I'm talking to Taylor. He tells me to be at a certain place, stage door 3 or something like that, at 8PM on the Saturday night of the Johnny Cash concert.

Four days later, I'm at stage door 3. I'm not alone. My two pals are with me. It's 7:55. There's a grey-haired cop looking very bored, guarding the stage door. We must have made a strange-looking trio. He doesn't ask us what we're doing there. I'm glad he doesn't, because I wouldn't know what to tell him. For all I know some guy is going to open the door, hand us two Johnny Cash ashtrays and some application forms to the Johnny Cash Fan Club, and say, "Enjoy the show."

I haven't told Bobby and Gordon anything except that we are going to see Johnny Cash live at Boston Garden. What could I tell them? I don't know what's going on here myself. Upstairs in Boston Garden, the lights dim, and from our spot down below, in the runway, we can hear some music begin. Fifteen thousand fans are screaming and applauding. A band is beginning to warm up . Bobby and Gordon are restless. They want to know why we're "down in the cellar." They've asked me 10 times already why I've given each of them a little pad and a pen, since neither of them can read or write.

My heart is heavy. I look at my watch; it's almost ten past eight. Well, it seemed like a good idea, I think. It was worth a try. I take each of my pals by the arm, and begin to head up into the Garden proper. A voice behind me says, "Dan McCullough?"

I turn around. The guy in the doorway repeats the question. I nod my head. He beckons us. He leads us backstage to a spot near the main stage. "Wait here," he says. We wait. As we are waiting, I can still hear the warm-up band upstairs on stage. My back is to a dressing room area. My two pals are facing me. They are not having a good time. They are bored and confused. A minute later, I'm reviewing my first aid training, because it's clear that both Bobby and Gordon have gone into some sort of aphasiac seizure at the same time. Their eyeballs are frozen on an object behind me. I turn around. The object says, "Hi, Dan, I'm Johnny Cash."

I'll never forget him. He treated those two kids as if they were the co-owners of the biggest music production studio in Nashville. I stood to the side; it was their show. The three of them talked as if they were just three guys back in their neighborhood. They told him about the special schools they went to; he told them bus and airplane stories. He spent half an hour with them. I just could not believe this was happening. Soon his people were calling him; it was show time, time for us go. As they shook hands in parting, Bobby said, "I say a prayer for you every night, Johnny."

Cash looked like someone had punched him in the stomach. Then Gordon hit him with a left hook: "I don't pray for you every night, Johnny, but just on Sunday, when I go with my mom." Cash couldn't speak. His eyes filled up. He looked at me, his jaw was quivering. He reached over, took me by the arm, and shook my hand. "Thanks, Dan," he said, "Thanks very much."

I was biting my lip to keep from…well, keep from making a fool of myself. I just kept nodding my head as Cash shook my hand. I didn't feel much like talking.

We turned and walked away. Cash hollered after us, "What song would you boys like to hear?" Bobby and Gordon said at

TWO GUYS – FOR A LIFETIME

The phone call I got in the middle of the night is one I'll always remember. Twenty years later – in 2002 – I wrote a column about what that phone call symbolized to me.

There is a category of people, usually a small group of old, and I mean old, friends. These are people who know your history, know your failures as well as your victories. People who knew you when. I'm blessed with a handful of such people. The number can certainly be tallied on one, maybe two, hands. One of those is Mo MacDonough.

Garrett Blair MacDonough (I've always known him as "Mo,") lives in Point Judith, Rhode Island, down in the fishing village of Galilee. For several years, back in the '60s, he and I worked together there as commercial fishermen. Before that, when we were 14 or 15 years old, we worked together as staff members at Camp Yawgoog, a big boy scout camp over in Rockville, up against the Connecticut border.

He was in his twenties when he and Sandra, and baby Scott, their firstborn, moved down to Point Judith. They've been there ever since. After Scott was born, they had four more children: Paul, Enoch, Melissa, and Daniel, the youngest. I remember the night that Daniel was born, a little over 20 years ago. The phone rang in my house here on Cape Cod. It was late. I grappled for the phone on the nightstand in the darkness of the bedroom. It was Mo. Now understand that Mo doesn't do small talk. He always calls with something specific in mind. And he never introduces himself to me on the phone. He just starts talking.

"How're ya doin'?" the voice says on the other end of the line. Of course, I recognize his voice, even though I'm half asleep.

"Fine," I say. "What's up?"

"Sandra had the baby."

"Oh, good," I say.

"Yup, a little boy," Mo offers.

"Everybody OK?" I ask.

"Yup, just fine."

"Good, good," I say.

There's a pause in the conversation. Then he asks me if there's anything else I want to know. This seems like a strange question, but I'm half awake, and I'm sure Mo has had a few celebratory cigars, and maybe even a couple of beers, so I humor him and ask how much the baby weighs. He tells me. I make some comment about it being a good healthy weight, trying to sound as if I know something about babies. Then, the pause in the conversation again.

"Don't you want to know anything else?" he says.

"Uh, not really," I say.

"Don't you want to know what we're going to name him?"

I recover quickly. In the middle of the night, with the alarm set for five a.m., I think to myself: who cares what they're going to name this damned kid? But I humor him, and appear interested. "Oh, yeah, sure, what are you going to name him?"

"Daniel John" Mo says. "After you."

I didn't go back to sleep very quickly after that conversation ended, but lay there in bed, looking up at the lights and shadows on the ceiling, thinking about a newborn baby lying in his little bed in the darkened maternity ward of South County hospital, in Wakefield, RI, and me lying in the dark of my bedroom 100 miles away, thinking about his name, probably written in big letters with a black felt-tip marker on a piece of wide white adhesive tape and slapped on the foot of his crib.

"Daniel John." My name, his name.

I thought, as lay there, of how few people there were on earth that I would ever even think of naming a child after. I'd only had one child, and I named him Daniel John, too. But not after myself; after my own father, a man I loved above all men. And, of course, I thought as I lay there of Mo and me, and our friendship, and how very much we loved each other. I mean, how highly could you regard a man that you would name your last child after him?

So that was 20 years ago. The other night, the phone rang at my house; I picked it up.

"Hey, how's it goin'?" he said.

"Good, how you doin'?"

Mo explained that he had to do a week's refresher course to keep up his 1000-ton (or something like that) Coast Guard Captain's license to skipper big fishing boats or tugboats. There's not much that he hasn't done on the sea. He's run big fishing boats of all kinds, as well as tugboats, barges, dredges, and little lobster boats.

"The course is being given in Barnstable. That's near you, right?"

"Yeah," I said. "The college is in Barnstable."

"It lasts five days – Monday through Friday," he said.

"I wonder if I could bunk with you for the week? You know, save me a few bucks?"

We made plans for him to come on a Sunday, and stay as long as he wanted. And so he arrived on Sunday the 13th, sea bag in hand, and was out the door early Monday morning, off to his first day of class.

The program over in Hyannis went from the Ramada Inn, back and forth to the Barnstable Fire Academy up behind the airport. I think he said there were about 15 guys in the class.

Mo is exactly my age. We have the same nose, the same

blue eyes, same complexion and silhouette, a 500-lb. pair of bookends. When we were fishing together years ago, many people thought that we were brothers, our last names: McCullough and MacDonough and full-bearded faces were so similar.

We're both still in pretty good physical condition, Mo getting his exercise outside in the air, cutting up fish, splicing up cable or pulling on ropes, while I get mine in closed buildings with barbells and dumbbells. We never were, nor are we now, a couple of guys that most people would think of pushing around.

But were still not young, and the program he was in involved things like going into burning structures with air masks on and putting out the fire, jumping into the water fully clothed and rescuing himself, crawling around on hands and knees pulling gear along the ground, etc. When he got back to my house at night, usually around 7, he was pretty beat up. He'd have a bowl of ice cream; I'd have some cheese and crackers. We'd sit on the big leather couch by the fireplace for maybe an hour, and get the weather for the next day (all old sailors get the weather for the next day just before they go to bed). He'd clump his way upstairs; I'd put out the lights downstairs, head for my bed, and we'd both be asleep by 9.

In the morning, I'd be up at 5, put on the coffee, and by around six, I'd hear his big boots clumping down the stairs, and he'd appear at the table, baseball hat on, plaid flannel shirt tucked into his canvas work pants, held up by bright red suspenders. We'd wrap our big hands around little coffee mugs and crunch toast as we quietly talked about our schedules for that day, and then he'd step out into the yard for a cigarette, while I cleaned up the galley.

On Saturday, he proudly displayed his certificates of completion, looking like four or five engraved college degrees.

We gassed up my truck and went up to Provincetown; he wanted to inspect the fishing fleet there. We stopped to review the fleet at Wellfleet on the way up. We talked to a couple of fishermen at each place, had a couple of beers at the Governor Bradford Inn, and headed home.

As we pulled up onto the highway one guy asked the other guy, "You got any regrets?" and two old friends talked about that subject for the hour ride back to Orleans. Those are the kinds of conversations we have.

And then on Sunday, there we were standing in my driveway, him loading his gear for the trip home. We hugged each other long and hard, and then he slid behind the wheel, backed around in the driveway, and drove out, his brake lights blinking just once as he made the turn onto the street.

And then he was gone, leaving me standing in the yard recalling a day, over 30 years ago, when I packed up my gear, beginning the next chapter in my life, and left Point Judith. There is a long mile-long straight road which locals call "The Escape Road," built so that traffic could "escape" the fishing village in case of a hurricane. It runs uphill from Galilee, so that, at the top of the road, you can look in your rearview mirror and see the whole village laid out below and behind you.

I stopped my truck at the top of the hill that day and stepped out into the crisp March air. I knew what I was leaving behind, and I was terribly afraid that one of those things might be Mo MacDonough.

But a week ago today, after he left my house, I stood alone in my driveway, very grateful that never happened.

SOME SPECIAL FISHERMEN

For many years, the captains of the Rock Harbor fishing fleet of charter boats in Orleans gave up a day of business to take a group of special needs citizens out fishing. I'd usually write a column about it. This is a column from 1996.

I suppose your first clue that something special might be going that day might have come to you as you drove through Orleans early this past Wednesday morning.

If you had looked carefully at the Red Balloon Toy Store right in the middle of town, you would have seen Paul Jeffrey, the proprietor, helping Barbara Woodland and Debbie Donaldson load a truckful of multicolored balloons into the back of Barbara's vehicle. Dozens and dozens of the latex spheres squeaked, bounced and jiggled as the two women packed their lighter-than-air cargo.

And, as she does every year, Woodland offers Jeffrey money for the cargo of balloons, and, as he does every year, he declines and waves them off. He knows where they're going this morning, and his thoughts and best wishes go with them.

Down at Rock Harbor in Orleans, the two women begin at the south end of the harbor and, one by one, they tie the balloons to the railing that runs the length of the west end of the harbor. It takes a few minutes, but when they are done, and the gentle westerly breeze flicks its tongue on each balloon, the whole place is transformed into a place of joy, of lightness, of frivolity. It's not just a drab fishing harbor any more; it's a place for a carnival, for laughter and children's voices.

But the laughter and children's voices are not here yet. The parking lot is still relatively quiet, but the air is thick with the sort of suspense and tension that is felt before any great event. One of your first clues as to what is happening here might be the big yellow banner being stretched across the after part of Buddy Wilson's boat, the "High Calibre." In big blue letters across the banner it says, "Rock Harbor Special Olympics - WELCOME."

Up in the parking lot, Capt. Dick Woodland is standing at the back of his red truck (formerly loaded with balloons) with his wife Barbara, the balloon lady. His red-hulled boat, the "Madame B."bobs in its slip below, as his mate, Paul Plansky, and his junior mate, Brendan Adams, begin to prepare the fishing gear for today's expedition.

Slowly, the parking lot begins to fill with vans and station wagons, each filled with Special Olympians. The excitement builds as these special people spread across the walkways, ramps and docks of the harbor. The only people here today are people who are here to be part of this special day. There are no people here today who expect to be able to hire a boat to go fishing. If you talked to any of these captains over the winter and tried to hire a boat for July 17th, you'd be wasting your time.

Even if you showed up here with a fistful of $100 bills and tried to negotiate with Don Walwer, Captain of the "Terry II," Steve Peters on the "Nekton," or Art Hayes on the "Captain Cook," they'd just smile at you and tell you that your money was no good today. Good yesterday. Good tomorrow. But no good today. For this day is the 13th annual Rock Harbor Special Olympics, a day when serious businessmen, running sport fishing charter boats, give a whole day of their lives and their businesses to the Special Olympics.

Down the ramps they come, some with canes, others in wheelchairs. The folks fishing here are visibly different. Visibly special. Some have braces on limbs; others have physical and cognitive differences that would make them stand out in a crowd. But not today. There are no differences here today.

Everyone is special.

By 10:30, it seems that this utter chaos of chatter and laughter nervous energy will never result in any kind of formal organized reality. Dennis O'Connell, who, together with Dick Woodland, is mainly responsible for the organization of this thing for the past 13 years, is pacing around with a clipboard in his hand, trying to distribute the boat assignments for the 150 or so people who are going to be boarding boats here in the next half hour. O'Connell is clutching the clipboard as if it were a life preserver from one of the boats, and he were adrift at sea.

But, as it has for the past 13 years, it all falls together, and soon the folks are loaded on the boats and the fleet of 23 boats from Orleans, Dennis, Wellfleet and Barnstable, sails out in single file, horns blowing, streamers flying. All the energy from the parking lot has been transferred to the boats. The folks back on shore watching this spectacle are waving, and taking pictures, but they are mostly quiet, aware that they are in the presence of something very special, something bigger than a game, something bigger than a competition or a contest.

As one of the boats pulls out, a man is aboard with his brother, one of the Special Olympians. He looks up to a local woman he knows; she is standing along the railing looking down on the harbor. He speaks to her and waves, making some light-hearted remark about the spectacle unfolding here. She doesn't respond; her lips are pursed shut and she is staring straight ahead, shaking her head, her eyes rimmed with tears at what she is perceiving. She is not alone. All along the railing of the harbor, dozens of people are overcome with the reality here.

Out on the waters of Cape Cod Bay, the next few hours are filled with screams of joy and delight as everyone - everyone -

catches a fish. Sort of a miracle of the boats and the fishes. By 3:00 the boats are back in, discharging their special passengers and loads of bluefish.

Parents, guardians, family and friends all welcome the successful fishermen back from their annual trip. Everyone gets a special certificate of participation, and a new fishing hat imprinted with this year's date and logo. There are little trophies and awards given out. Then the tempo begins to slow down. The vans and wagons begin to load up their tired Olympians, the captains and mates wash down their boats and stow the fishing gear, and soon the parking lot is quiet again.

Two pretty salty looking grey-bearded guys are leaning against a pickup truck in the parking lot. The flotilla of fishing boats is now settling in on the falling afternoon tide. One speaks to the other, gesturing with his chin toward the empty parking lot. "Some people say those people are a gift from God, you know." The other guy doesn't speak, just turns, looks his friend in the eye, and says nothing. The first guy speaks again: "To help us be the best we can be," he says, staring back into the eyes of his friend.

The second guy is still silent, but he turns away and casts his glance out over the water to the north where, on a day like today, a man could see pretty far... probably all the way to the horizon.

A COUPLE FACES THE WINDS OF CHANGE

This column, published in 2003, points out the courage of a young couple making lifelong commitments in the face of a world of change and chaos, nothing enduring or constant, with the possible exception of love for each other and the love of God.

I was sitting in the tenth row of the pews in one of the oldest churches in America last weekend, the First Parish Church of Cambridge, in Harvard Square. You know the church; you've driven by it many times. It's the big church at the corner of Church Street and Massachusetts Avenue, directly across the street from Harvard Yard.

The community here was founded in the same year as Harvard University: 1636. The building I was sitting was built in 1833.

The pastor here, Reverend Thomas Mikelson, was speaking. A man beloved by his community, he had the attention of every member of the congregation standing here today as he called for God's blessing upon the young couple standing before him. When he was finished, he looked up at the congregation, and invited them to be seated.

And then he gestured to me with a subtle nod of his head and, as the others took their seats, I stepped out into the aisle and slowly began to walk alone to the front of the church. When I got to the front, I turned to the left, walked a few feet and getting to the bottom of the steps leading up to the pulpit, I began to climb the stairs.

I had forgotten how high above the main floor level the pulpits in these old churches are. To stand there is to capture the eyes of every person assembled in front of you, right to the back row.

I looked out over the congregation, and then down at the bride Kate Willrich, beautiful and beaming with love. Next to her was her groom, Erik Nordahl. As I looked down at him, our eyes met for a moment and I reflected about the journey that had brought me to be standing in this place on Saturday the 4th of January, 2003.

In the late 1980s, Erik had been my student at Cape Cod Community College. I think the first course he took with me was a survey course in western religions. He was a superior student, and did well. He signed up for other courses with me after that one.

Now, I'll tell you something that most of my students already know: I'm not a guy who is interested in being buddy-buddy with his students. I don't care if they like me or not, and during the first lecture each semester, I tell them this. I tell them that I have enough damned friends, and the last thing I need are any new ones. Actually, I'd like to get rid of a few.

But despite my best efforts, some students become lifelong friends, long after they've left Cape Cod. Erik is one of these. After getting his degree here, he went on to Stonehill College. We kept in touch while he was there, through phone calls, e-mails, and occasional visits. When he finished at Stonehill, he went on to law school in Delaware, subsequently passing the Massachusetts bar and becoming a practicing attorney here.

When he came back to Massachusetts, we kept in closer touch, having lunch or just sitting around talking. He has two sisters, but no brothers, so I became a sort of older brother to him serving as his confidant, counselor and friend, and this friendship blossomed as the years went by. He is the same age as my own son, and I've often referred to him as "my

Swedish son."

Erik is a man of high principles; after practicing law for a few years, he took a much lower-paying job working as an advocate for handicapped citizens. Having great affection for his Barnstable alma mater, he currently serves on the board of directors of the Cape Cod Community College Educational Foundation.

As a single guy, his standards for women were so high that I was sure he'd be a bachelor all his life. He'd dated women on and off; I knew some of them. But things just never clicked. Like I say, he had very high standards, and I just never thought he'd find her.

But one day in 2001, he called me and we made plans to have lunch. As we walked to the little corner table at the Yardarm Restaurant in Orleans, John Sully, the owner followed us. He greeted Erik; we exchanged a few words, and then we were alone. I know this young man very well; he had something heavy on his mind.

"What's up?" I said.

"Dan," he said with a very serious look on his face, "I've met someone. A woman." And then the serious look on his face began to dissolve like an ice cream cone on a hot July day in Edgartown. By the time he uttered the next sentence, his face was containing a smile the size of the grill on a 1954 Buick. "Her name is Kate – Kate Willrich."

And, of course, it wasn't many weeks before I was sitting having lunch with Kate and Erik. Seventeen seconds after meeting her, I could see why he was so smitten. She was indeed a beautiful human being, and a beautiful woman to go along with it.

It wasn't long after we had lunch that Erik, on his first visit to meet Kate's family in California, cleared his throat after dinner with the Willrich family, and said he had something to say. He slid his chair back, knelt down in front of Kate, and asked her to marry him.

"There wasn't a dry eye at the table," her brother told me last week.

The next year, they asked me to be the homilist, or main speaker, at their wedding. So there I was, a week ago yesterday, standing in the pulpit looking down at the two of them. I have never known two people more in love; I have never felt so good about a marriage. Never.

As I gathered my thoughts and looked out over the congregation, a latecomer came through the doors at the back of the church, and the cacophony and confusion of Saturday afternoon in Harvard Square was evident for just a few seconds, and then, as the door closed, it was gone. I knew that if the door opened again, even a few seconds later, the scene would be different.

So I started with the observation that the world outside us is, according to Hindu thinking, "maya," or illusion. I pointed out that modern physicists say the same thing: that the physical world, the world outside is chaos and change, never being what it seems to be. I reminded them that Jesus had said the same thing in telling us that the kingdom of God is within us.

I told them that the only truth they would find would be through their love for each other, and God's love for them. All the rest was, as the Hindus say, "maya."

As my 15 minutes came to a close, I looked down at this beautiful couple, and felt humbled by their courage in the face of the world's chaos to dare to make the commitment they were making here today.

And I said to them and to the congregation behind them, that each of us might not find the truth through love and God, but we surely would find it no place else.

FORGIVENESS

Reading this tragic story in 1987 moved me very deeply to think about the nobility and compassion – and difficulty – involved in the human act of forgiveness.

There is a place in our modern society where ancient Judeo-Christian principles and modern psychological theories meet in agreement. The place I have in mind is upon the issue of forgiveness.

Jewish scholars point to Deuteronomy, where Jahweh reserves vengenace to Himself. I can remember Nathan Fink, my best friend's dad, telling me when I was a teenager, of the old Jewish saying, "A man who hates is like a man who has swallowed a stone." A powerful metaphor, it has stayed with me all my life. The life of Jesus of Nazareth was, of course, a living statement of the principle of forgiveness. A key element of The Lord's Prayer is the petition that God treat us in the same manner that we forgive others.

Contemporary psychology is rife with this notion. Therapists spend hours, indeed years, trying to get people to allow for the mistakes, neglect, and even the deliberate vicious treatment, received at the hands, or from the psyche, of parents, peers, ex-spouses, lovers, or neighbors. Patients in therapy today are told to let go of this resentment, this hate, this stone that they have swallowed, and get on with their lives.

Many of you might recognize this as one of the key elements in what is perhaps the most successful of all modern healing programs, Alcoholics Anonymous.

The word here is forgiveness. Eleven letters long - a big word.

I thought a lot about this word when I heard a story this

week of how two citizens of the Commonwealth recently met each other on the evening of September 28 at the Sunrise Shopping Center in Lowell:

CITIZEN #1: Marie Tousignant, 54. Widow, mother of seven, grandmother of six. Has worked two jobs to support her family since her husband, their father and grandfather, died of heart trouble 14 years ago, leaving her with seven children under the age of eighteen. One of the Tousignant children, Mary, named after her mother, is a retarded adult and the apple of her mother's eye. In addition to working two jobs, Marie finds time to be active in the Association for Retarded Citizens of Greater Lowell, and in the Retarded Adult Rehabilitation Association of Lowell. She takes great pride in Mary's achievements, and the two of them travelled to Colorado last year so Mary could compete in the Special Olympics there. She won a bronze medal.

A woman. An American woman. A beautiful woman. More beautiful than any blow-dried, eyebrow-plucked, tooth-capped, air-headed "beauty" that you'll see strutting across the Miss America stage in Atlantic City this fall.

CITIZEN #2: Robert Petalas, 39. Residence: a lean-to built in the woods nearby the shopping center. Unemployed for at least the past six years. Known drug abuser. Narcotics arrest record in Lowell. Outstanding warrants and defaults on bail bonds in Springfield and Worcester. Dismissed from a shelter of last resort for alcohol and drug abusers in August, for allegedly bringing opium into the shelter. On the day he met Marie Tousignant, Lowell Police found dozens of bottles of prescription drugs in his lean-to in the nearby woods.

THE MEETING: Marie Tousignant stops at the Sunrise Shopping Center on her way home from work. She puts her groceries into the car, puts her car into reverse, and starts to back out. According to police, Robert Petalas comes up to the car, opens the door, and, in an attempt to prevent her purse from being snatched, she is dragged out of the car, her head and neck landing behind one of the wheels as the car rolls backward. She is pronounced dead at the scene.

You can picture the scene, if you wish. I'd rather not. It was suggested to me by the friend who told me the story that maybe the bronze medal was in the pocketbook. I'd rather not think about that, either.

So, forgiveness. Yeah, I thought about it a lot this week. I thought about the dead woman's house with the Special Olympics trophies up on the mantle by the dining room mirror, and I thought about the sudden silence that slashed into the life of the Tousignant family that day, and I thought about the tears in the eyes of a retarded woman/child standing at her mother's grave, and I thought about Robert Petalas, and then I thought more about forgiveness.

And I realized that although we may know in our hearts and our minds that it is the right thing, sometimes it must be so very, very, hard to do.

THE WOMAN IN THE BLUE HOUSECOAT

You know how sometimes you just catch a glimpse of something, a quick flash or glance, and that image stays with you? That's what happened to me driving by a house in Orleans in 1987.

No scallops. Not this year. So I did what a bunch of other guys did this week - put away the scallop gear. It's really not much of a job for small-timers such as I: some line, some hardware, scallop drags, some wire basket, a short mast and a couple of stays, - that's it.

It's funny, but when there are scallops, it seems to hold off winter a few more weeks. When there are none, fall is over and winter is here. As my friend and fishing partner, Bobby Wilcox, a Cape Cod native, says, "There are five seasons: spring, summer, fall, scallop and winter." The scallop season seems to form a buffer between fall and winter. When there are no scallops, the buffer is gone, winter arrives and it is longer than it might have been.

The boat doesn't get put away yet, though. The boat gets left out until mid-December just in case....well, let's just say that the boat gets left out. To put the boat up for the winter would really be an admission that it truly is over. I don't do that until the days start to get longer on December 21st.

So I come back into the warm house with armsful of paraphernalia from the boat: fishing tackle from the summer bluefishing follies, extra lines for the scallop gear, a gaff, life jacket, boots and oilers, gloves, etc., etc. The articles in my hands are cold with the chill of November. Bringing them into the warm house is like bringing in winter. The house is colder already.

It's a simple calculus to me: a day in which one walks by this gear stored in the back hall is a winter day. Storing this gear this early makes winter longer because there are more days to walk past this stuff in the hall than if the gear were in the boat, working on scallops. Like I said, it's simple.

Anyway, I'm going over the waterproof pouch of documents from the boat: the registration, some identification, the commercial fishing permits. As I look at the commercial permits ($100 worth) and think about how I'm not going to pay for my permits this year with scallop money, I flash back to a day last spring - the day I drove around to get my permits.

You know how some events may be imprinted in your mind's eye like a snapshot? Maybe watching a friend falling off a dock into the water....Snap! The scene is imprinted in your mind forever. Years later you can see your friend, arms outstretched, mouth open, eyes wide.... Your child at a grade school concert. Snap! Your grandmother in her warm kitchen, wiping her hands on her apron. Snap! The look on a doctor's face as he came to give bad news to your family. Snap!

Well, as I was saying, this past March I'm driving around to local town halls to get my commercial scalloping permits. It's a beautiful spring day, one of those days around the equinox when it's unseasonably warm and thoughts of June blow in and out the open windows of my truck as I run my errands.

I'm driving down Meeting House Road, a quiet residential street that runs next to the Federated Church in East Orleans, and I see a rescue truck pulled up on the lawn of a house up ahead on the right, not far from the old cemetery there. I slow to a crawl, and as I get closer, I see two EMT's wheeling a stretcher with elderly man aboard down the walkway from the house to the truck. A tall, slim, grey-haired woman in a long blue housecoat stands by the walk: her elbows are together at her waist; her ten fingers are together at her mouth. She might be praying.

She stares at the man on the stretcher. The bright blue of her housecoat stands in contrast to the brown leafless bushes behind her in the yard. Snap! This picture is framed in the windshield of my truck. My knuckles are in the bottom of the picture, at the top of the steering wheel; my lobster gauge is hanging from the rear-view mirror in the middle of the picture, together with a faded red necktie. The permits I now hold in my hands on this chilly November day lie on the dashboard in the warm March sun.

That picture which snapped into my memory has stayed with me these past months and it comes back to me today, as I look at the government documents in my hands, and think about scallops and winter.

But this is not the first time that etched scene has popped back into my consciousness. It came back to me in June, when I drove by that house a few months after my first encounter with the rescue team. I noticed that the grass had not been cut recently and a hole had been torn in the screen door to the porch. It came back to me in October, when I drove by and saw that the yard and driveway were covered with unraked leaves and the door to the mailbox at the edge of the road was hanging open on one hinge, swinging in the fall breeze.

So, yeah, the winter's going to be a little longer for me this year because of the scallops and all, but I think that it's going to be a lot longer for some people for reasons which are not so clear – for people like the woman in the blue housecoat.

CONSIDERING A FINAL GOODBYE

Every so often, I pull out a 25-year-old manila folder and consider destroying it. This is an account of my 2013 decision-making process.

A beautiful day – this past Wednesday. The sun was higher in the sky than it has been since September, and the temperature flirting with 50. Rare tiny pockets of snow were hidden in shady crannies of north-facing buildings at Cape Cod Community College. Spring on a college campus is a time of nostalgia, especially so for an old academic bear such as I. Walking across campus, my eyes squinting against the bright sun, I thought of the semesters of my life I had spent on college campuses.

Getting to my office, I put down my backpack and fished my key out of my vest pocket. As I opened the door, a blast of heat swept over me. One wall of my office is about 50 square feet of south-facing glass. Closed and locked from sunrise, the office was a thermal trap of solar radiation. It felt good – for a minute or two - but soon I went to the window and cranked it open to the fresh air. A few small dry leaves blew in as the window swung open for the first since October.

I dropped into my chair and looked around the office. People who know me well can make a pretty good guess as to what my office looks like: scattered, disordered, unmanageable chaos, sort of the academic equivalent of city ravaged by a decade of civil war. Notice that I said that was what my office "looks like." In reality, I pretty much know where everything is. But now and then, every five or six years, usually in the spring, I look around the room and think to myself: I've got to tidy up this place. It was just noon. I had a free hour before a 1:00 panel discussion I was scheduled to be involved in, so

I reached up and pulled a handful of old file folders sticking out from the end of a bookcase in front of me, you know, to maybe begin just a few minutes of the big cleanup. I just held the old folders in my lap and thought. When I think of cleaning up my office, I always think of the Greek hero and demigod Hercules.

In ancient mythology, Hercules was the son of the god Zeus and a mortal woman. Famous for strength, he was reputed to be the strongest of all mortals, and even stronger than some of the gods. In the Greek tradition, Hercules is the only human who became a god after his death. Zeus' wife Hera, a nasty and vindictive character, was jealous of Hercules and made him temporarily insane. In his madness, he murdered his own children. When the madness had passed, he went to the Delphic Oracle, the wisest of women, and asked how he could atone for such a horrible act.

She told him to go to the king and do whatever he ordered him to do, and then his horrible deeds would be atoned for. The king set 12 very difficult tasks for Hercules. The fifth task was to clean out the Augean stables where over 1000 head of cattle lived and defecated daily. The stables had not been cleaned in over 30 years and Hercules task was to clean all of the stables out in one day. So when I sit in my office and look around, thinking of reorganizing it, I always think of Hercules and the Augean Stables.

I fingered the folders in my hands. Some were empty; I put them aside to be reused. Some had old outdated materials in them: ten-year old schedules, worthless memos from people no longer working at the college, syllabi from courses no longer being taught, etc.

And then I came to an old manila folder that I recognized immediately. The folder was dog-eared and worn. The outside was stained with what looked like coffee stains, maybe cola.

I knew this folder very well. I knew that it was not empty. I knew exactly what was inside it. The materials in this folder were several decades old. It could have dated back to the 1980s. Every few years I would come across this folder, hold its contents in my hands and read the pages, and then put the folder back into the random collection of old folders in the corner of the bookcase. I had not held the folder for several years. I opened it up.

Inside were two pieces of paper. The student had written her name on the top of both pages. A semester schedule of appointments with me was on the top page. The second page was an exam corrected with comments and a grade written in now-faded red ink, ready to be returned to the student. The first question had to do with the differences between the Mahayana and Theravada traditions in Buddhism. The second question concerned the Four Noble Truths of Buddhism. The last question on the back was about Zen Buddhism. The grade was 15 out of 20, a respectable "C."

The student's name was Lydia Gillis. Her handwriting was flamboyant and artistic, with sweeping circles under her "g"s, "j"s and "y"s. The "R"s "D"s and "B"s had large empty ovals in their script. I remember Lydia Gillis. I remember that, the day she took this exam in my hands, Lydia Gillis was killed in an accident on the way home from the college, leaving me and the exam waiting for her to come pick it up.

She would be a woman in her 40s today, I thought as I held the old pages in my hand, and asked once more, as I have for decades, why do I keep this folder? I had promised myself that once I knew the answer to that question, I would dispose of the folder and its contents.

Did I have the answer this time? I thought about it and then closed the folder and made a decision. I knew that it was the right thing to do.

_____ The Sea

TALKING TO SEA CREATURES

Peter Beamish is one of the most unforgettable characters I've ever met (and believe me: I've met a few). He sometimes sounded so crazy that he had to be sane. This 2002 column tells of my first encounter with him.

When I first met Peter Beamish, I immediately noticed how much he resembled, to me, the character of Oliver Sacks as played by Robin Williams in the movie "Awakenings." The round face, the thick glasses, the quick smile: they were all there.

It was a week ago today, and I was in the tiny fishing village of Trinity, halfway out the Bonavista Peninsula of Newfoundland, about 800 miles out to sea from Portland, Maine. Newfoundland isn't a little island like Nantucket, either; it's bigger than Ohio. And don't bother to look for Trinity on your map; you won't find it. You may find Trinity Bay, the size of one of the Great Lakes, but you won't find Trinity. The village of Trinity makes downtown Wellfleet look like Cleveland. Three or four churches, a couple of dozen houses, the blacksmith shop, theater, museum, sawmill, and a bunch of B&Bs; that's it. There's one winding road leading down to the village.

To get to Trinity, I had taken the bus from Hyannis to Logan Airport, flew to Halifax, Nova Scotia, connected with another flight to St. John's, Newfoundland, picked up a car at the airport and drove three or four hours, several hundred miles, along a variety of roads ranging from the six-lane Trans-Canada Highway to one-lane gravel roads. The temperature was perhaps ten degrees cooler than when I had left Cape Cod. In Newfoundland at this time of year, the highs are in the low

70s and the low in the 50s. It doesn't get much better than that. But there I was on a beautiful Sunday afternoon, the second Sunday in July, putting on the left-hand turn signal in my leased car as I came upon a simple green sign that said "TRINITY" with a small arrow at the bottom. I turned onto the road, and a half mile later I came over the crest of a hill, and there was the village laid out below me, snuggled up against the Atlantic Ocean.

Within ten minutes, I was standing in the front hall of the Village Inn, talking to Peter Beamish, Dr. Peter Beamish, actually, whale researcher and communications expert, and author of several books on communications between animals and humans. Early in our conversation, I mention Cape Cod; he responds with a sentence containing the term Woods Hole. Soon we're talking about whales and then on to communications. Not long after that, I'm out on the ocean with him in a small Zodiac gray rubber inflatable raft. He's got sound apparatus hanging over the edge of the boat, sending pings out to attract whales. He's standing up on the steering console peering out over the water. I'm standing next to him peering out too, not sure what I'm supposed to be looking for.

He's talking to himself. He's steering the boat with his feet. I'm wondering what the hell I'm doing out here, a long way from home. What is it about me that attracts people like Beamish to me, I wonder. But, soon enough, I realize that he's been talking to the whales as well as himself, for right up ahead of us rises a monstrous figure, a massive finback whale, the second largest animal on earth, larger than a giant dinosaur. The animal is about 80 feet long, as long as two trailer trucks, and weighs well over 100,000 lbs.

Off to our right, a humpback whale appears, really close to the boat. Then another, its mate, surges up right beside it.

These animals are right beside us. If I could secure my feet onto the boat somehow, I could reach out and touch them. I can see their eyes looking up at us as we move along with them, one on each side of the boat. Beamish is talking to them like you would talk to a pet dog. He's not even aware that I'm standing next to him. He's in his own world.

So am I. I've been among whales before. I've actually touched a whale in the wild once. But it was a small pilot whale in the middle of a big pod of whales. This is different. One of these animals could kill us with a single swipe of its tail, and yet I'm feeling no fear, as if I'm among friends.

"They know you're there," Beamish explains later as we sit in the small parlor at his inn. "They know you mean them no harm. They certainly know me." We've finished dinner together and the tiny village has quieted down. It's close to ten o'clock at night and it's still daylight outside, a function of our latitude and time zone.

"We share a biological rhythm with the whales," he explains. "We do that among ourselves, too. That's how people sometimes know that a loved one has died, thousands of miles away." He mentions a connection that he felt when we first talked. I don't admit it to him right then, but I felt the same connection. He pours another coffee, and the conversation goes on to the details of non-verbal communication, and then on to the communication skills of whales and humans. He explains that whales understand music. "They don't just listen to it," he says. "They understand it, like a composer understands it."

Now I know he's crazy. I've got to nip this conversation in the bud before it gets out of hand.

"Do you mean to tell me," I say, tapping the tablecloth with my index finger for emphasis, "That a whale can understand the sequences of chord progressions, thirds and fifths and

Pythagorean harmonics in a piece of music?"

"Oh sure," he says offhandedly.

"Do you mean," I ask him (just pulling two examples out of the air), "That a whale understands the chord progressions in say, Beethoven's Moonlight Sonata, or Tchaikovsky's First Piano Concerto?" (Reader: remember these two pieces of music).

"Oh certainly," he says. "They'd understand certain components of a piece of music better than others, but they'd understand it. Come on, I'll show you," he says standing up and heading for the stairs leading up to his residence above the dining room.

At the top of the stairs, he introduces me to his wife, who quickly disappears into another part of the house, as if Beamish bringing large strangers in the house at 10 o'clock at night is nothing new.

I follow him into a small sitting room. A small Yamaha concert piano is against the wall to our right. He sits down at the piano, gesturing to me to sit down in a nearby chair. I look up at the piano, and see something I will never forget. Up on the music stand above the keys are two pieces of sheet music: Beethoven's Moonlight Sonata, and Tchaikovsky's First Piano Concerto, incredibly enough, the very two pieces of music I had mentioned moments earlier while we were sitting downstairs.

I'm astonished, and I excitedly point this out to him, and he simply says, matter-of-factly, "Oh yeah, that's rhythm-based communication. You knew that these were the two pieces up here; you just weren't consciously aware of it."

He goes on to play the Tchaikovsky, and talking about whales, but I'm not listening to the music or him. I'm staring at the printed sheets, wondering which one of us is crazy and what might be the other things I know, but am not aware of.

PUTTING 180,000 BABIES TO BED

This 1988 column is as much a statement about the people of Orleans as is about the shellfish.

On a quiet night this week, about half an hour after sunset, I found myself in a work skiff in the upper reaches of Pleasant Bay, headed south toward Chatham. The sun had been down for awhile, but all of the land around me was still aglow in that incredible afterlight which occurs here in October.

When I see light such as that, where every detail of every branch on the crest of a hill against the horizon is carved in black, and the outline of the spars of every sailboat at its mooring is etched against the coral sky in the west, I wish that I were a painter or a photographer.

All of the land around the Bay was India ink black, but the sky and the water were still quietly on fire, with the sun, now well over the horizon, still transferring its glow to the sky over me, and the sky, in turn, transferring that glow to the glassy waters of Pleasant Bay. There was no other boat on the water tonight; the October chill and the time of day (or night) precluded the presence of pleasure boaters, and since there were no scallops this year, there would be no commercial scallopers out here either.

Besides, it is illegal to catch or transport scallops at night; the penalties are stiff. You could pay a hefty fine or even spend some time in prison, depending on the circumstances, for having a few pounds of scallops in your boat at this time of night. This thought did not escape me as I looked around the skiff and realized that there were, in the boat with me, approximately 180,000 scallops. In this boat with me tonight there were so many scallops that I didn't have room to sit anywhere, but had to stand. In the quiet night air, I could hear their little shells snapping against each other in a futile swimming motion which scallops use when they are in the water.

I couldn't even imagine what the prison term and fines might be for 180,000 (more or less) scallops. I guess I was a little nervous about this whole thing. I had never done anything like this before. Someone I trusted had really gotten me into this whole thing, I thought. I pulled my hooded yellow slicker tighter around my neck against the night air, and turned around to look over the stern of the boat.

What I saw would frighten any shellfish poacher. I was looking into the eyes of Larry Ellis, the Orleans Harbormaster and Shellfish Warden. I could see his uniform clearly in the fading light. He was steering his boat and looking me right in the eye. He wasn't smiling; he had the look of a man who was about to become engaged in some serious business. There was no sense in trying to explain anything to him; he knew why I was here, and he knew exactly what I was up to.

I think I'd better tell you how I got involved in this whole thing.

It all began very innocently. Looking back on the whole thing, I think that maybe it was really Ted Reynolds' fault. Ted is my friend. He lives in Truro. He's a builder. He's a nice guy. I like him.

Ted and I have one social habit in common: we both tend to speak slowly, with long pauses between sentences, sometimes between words. I think that people are always interrupting us, but they don't even know it - they think that we're done talking. The first time I met Reynolds, I liked him; he let me finish sentences. He liked me; I did the same. So, whenever we have a chance, we enjoy spending time together and talking. That's what we were doing when this whole thing began this week.

We were sitting in a local watering hole, the Land-Ho! in downtown Orleans. It was around dinnertime. I had finished my beer and was getting ready to leave when Ted ordered another round. (I think this is where it begins to become his fault.) We talked some more. Before I could finish that beer, Sandra Macfarlane, Orleans Town Biologist, burst into the restaurant, looked around quickly and spotted Reynolds and me at the bar. She was on us in a flash. She was desperate. She needed help.

This was her story: the town had ordered its fall supply of reseeding stock to plant scallops in the waters of Pleasant Bay. Through a mixup in transportation plans, the shellfish had arrived an half an hour ago at the airport in Hyannis. Her truck was running outside with the scallops on it. 180,000 of them, each as big as an M&M. They needed to get into the water as soon as possible. Larry Ellis, the aforementioned Shellfish Warden, was sitting at the dock at town landing with the engine to his boat running, waiting for the orphans to be delivered. Two able-bodied persons were needed to complete the mission. I looked at Reynolds; he looked at me. We both looked at Macfarlane. The next thing I was looking at was the parking lot. The next thing I knew, we were loading the 100-lb. boxes of scallops into Ellis' skiff.

So that's how I happen to be looking into the serious face of the shellfish warden. So, on with the story: we get to the place where Ellis and Macfarlane have decided will be the nursery for these little ones. The boat slows down, as landmarks are double-checked. This is it!

As Ellis slowly navigates the skiff in a weaving pattern over the area, Reynolds, Macfarlane and I broadcast the scallops, by hand, over the surface of the water. I begin to understand why this process is called "seeding." We are sprinkling the baby scallops over the water in exactly the same manner, and with the same hand and arm motions as the farmer plants grain. To look at our silhouettes, you could think that we were spreading grass seed.

The job was soon finished; it didn't take long. By this time, it was full-blown night. We were silent on the way home, there wasn't much to say. I had a feeling that the three other people in the boat might have been sharing some of the same feelings I had: the feeling of having done a necessary job, the feeling of having helped one of the visible cycles of nature (the two-year scallop cycle) continue, and the good feeling of knowing that we live in a part of the world here on the lower Cape, where a couple of municipal officials can, in two minutes at a local pub, get together a couple of volunteers to help, without asking any questions.

Under the streetlamp of the town landing we said goodnights and thank-yous. A few light-hearted comments were exchanged, trucks were started, taillights disappeared up Pond Road, and the night finally took over the dark waters of Pleasant Bay and Meetinghouse River. It must have looked much the same as it did 24 hours before. But I knew better.

Out in the cold dark water there were almost 200 thousand new baby animals, each struggling to live, each struggling to find a safe place for the Cape Cod winter. We four humans had changed this place, as humans change every place to which they go. But this time, the change had been for the better, and that felt good.

A VOWEL AWAY FROM ETERNITY

In 2013, I stood by a fisherman's memorial at Point Judith, Rhode Island, and read the name of one of the dead men inscribed in stone in front of me. But is wasn't just any old name.

I was born within half a mile of salt water and today, these decades later, I live that same distance from the sea. Before I went to sea, I had spent a lot of my young years living a kind of nomad life: hitchhiking across America twice before I was 20 years old, working with migrant farm workers on the Mexican border, driving on road for a couple of years in the Teamsters' Union, going to Key West with plans of moving to Cuba to fight with Castro. My buddies who had settled down, taken serious career jobs, gotten married, had children, envied my free spirit, and many people who knew me were sure I would never stop being the gypsy wanderer. It all looked good from the outside, but I was incomplete, not sure myself what I was doing, or where I was going.

Then in 1961, I found myself back at the edge of the sea, in the fishing village of Galilee at Point Judith in Narragansett Rhode Island. Years previously, when I was 14 years old, I had worked with a buddy of mine, Moe MacDonough, at Camp Yawgoog, a boy scout camp down on the Connecticut border. While still in his teens, he had become a fisherman at Point Judith, and we had sort of kept in touch. A close friend of mine, Paul Gorman, a fellow wanderer I had known since high school, had also settled there as a commercial fisherman, and he had convinced me to give it a try. He put me in touch with Jim McCauley, captain of the big trawler, "Jerry and Jimmy"; he hired me on Gorman's recommendation, and my life changed.

Commercial fishing was at the time and is still today the most dangerous job in America. But we were young and that fact was just a statistic. When you're 21 years old, you know you're going to live forever, and it's the other guys who are going to get killed on the job, no matter how dangerous. So although I was aware of the dangers involved, I kept at it, and as years went by, I changed. I believe much of that change was a result of working on a job where you could really get killed. After about five years, I was done rambling and ready to settle down. I left fishing, went to graduate school in Boston, got married, had a baby, started paying a mortgage, and even took a job as a technical writer in a big corporation out on Route 128.

I still kept in touch with Moe MacDonough (he was in my wedding party) and Paul Gorman (we became even closer friends over the years). Both those guys stayed fishing in Point Judith, and we stayed in touch.

This past Monday, I got up early, had some breakfast, went downtown and gassed up my truck at Bill's Sunoco in Orleans, and pulled up on the highway headed west to Point Judith. Two hours later, Moe and I are standing in the morning sun of his driveway in the fishing village at Point Judith, our arms around each other.

We had lunch, and then worked our way out to the very end of Point Judith, by the lighthouse and the Coast Guard Station. We parked my truck by the Point Judith Fisherman's Memorial there, three polished granite stones overlooking the Atlantic. The middle stone has engraved the poem "Sea Fever" by John Masefield ("I must go down to the sea again, to the lonely sea and sky..."). The single stones on either side are engraved with the names of Point Judith fishermen who have died while fishing. Underfoot, etched in stone, is a compass rose. We stand silently next to one another, each in our own thoughts. I'm amazed that I personally knew at least a third of the 56 names carved on the stones in front of me:

Bruce Loftes, blonde curly-haired kid, we crewed together for his father, Harold Loftes, on the "Miss Point Judith." Harold, now close to 90, is still fishing. Joey Fitzpatrick, a kid from Warwick, RI. We knew each other before we came to fishing. Hank Winter and Ken Winter, two uncles of Butch Winter, a guy I also fished with. Franny Webb, another young guy I hung around with: we shot plenty of pool together. George Garrett, a drinking buddy. Fred Rose, a Block Islander, washed overboard one winter day. More and more names...

Toward the end, the names on the stone become more familiar, more personal. Paul Gorman, my close friend who got me my first job here. Herb Spinney, like a big brother to me; I lived in his house with him and his family while I was fishing, also washed overboard on a cold North Atlantic winter night. Then Scott MacDonough, the first-born son of the man standing next to me. I remember the day I raced to Point Judith to be with Moe when Scott was killed on the boat, not far from shore. I unconsciously whisper his name out loud; Moe and I exchange glances, then look back down.

The only name I reach down and touch is a name on the left-hand stone, not far from Moe's son's name. I run my fingers over the letters: DON McCULLOUGH, the name of a man I never met, a man not known by many people in Point Judith at the time. I had taken a trip off from a boat I had been working on; I think it was the "Rose Marie V"; I forget. But the captain, Dave Lagasse, had hired this guy to take my place.

So death brushes by all of us now and then; sometimes we are aware of it – sometimes not. Sometimes it brushes as close as a vowel on a stone memorial. Today, June 30th, is my

A TINY SEA CREATURE DIES

As I came upon the needless death of this tiny creature, I was very moved, but I couldn't bring to mind what my feelings were. When that happens, a writer sits down and begins writing until the story comes out, as it did in this piece from 2002.

We are blessed to live in such a place as Cape Cod where, if you are of such a mind, you can go to the sea in the early morning, look to the east, and actually observe the very moment when the day begins. Sunsets are beautiful here, as well, especially in September and October, but I much prefer the beginning of things rather than the endings. So, it's my habit to walk the beach in the early morning.

I usually start a little bit before sunrise. At the moment when the day begins, I like to be in a place where I can hear the surf pounding, taste the salt air, and feel the wind on my face. When the sun first peers over the horizon, somewhere out in the Atlantic, my six-foot shadow can be 100 feet long. If I raise my walking stick over my head and look to the west, the shadow gets even longer.

I suppose this affection for beginnings is why I was touched by the evidence of an ending that I came upon one morning last week. The incident has stayed with me like a tick on a moose, a remora on a shark. I can't seem to shake it.

I had been a little bit less than halfway out on a three-mile trek when I came upon the thing. In my walk this morning, I had abandoned the outer beach for a sandy track behind the dunes. This time of year, the road here is used mostly by fishermen and surfers trying to get to a more isolated spot on the beach to do their thing.

We writers are always looking. Our favorite subjects are, of course, people. But with no people around, we look anyway.

At anything. When I'm hiking, I'm looking across the marsh for deer, looking ahead on the beach or the trail for skunk or raccoon, looking in the air for osprey, harriers, red tail hawks, buzzards or the rare by occasional eagle, looking behind me for Mr. Coyote who likes to come around behind me. He's neither threatened nor threatening; he just stands in the trail I've just covered and watches me. After our eyes meet, he trots off into that place where coyotes go when we are not watching them.

But most of the time, for some reason, I'm looking down. It may be that in the pre-dawn light, a hiker needs to watch his step. It may be that I do my prayers and meditation in the morning while hiking and looking down seems to be the body posture of such behavior. It may be that, over the years, I've found a lot of neat stuff underfoot while hiking on the beach trail. You know, fishing lures, gloves, coins, small tools, etc.

But I think the reason I'm looking down most of the time is because of the life there. Depending on the season, there are June bugs, crickets, small snakes, the tracks of raccoons, coyotes, rabbits. In the fall and winter, the deer come out of where they hide all summer and sometimes I actually come upon the tracks of what can only be a small herd of deer.

It was while I was looking down on that day last week when I saw it. Or what was left of it.

Actually, I saw its trail first. And I was confused. My first thought was that a little kid had been walking along the trail the day before and she had a little stick she was playing with. And as she walked along, she made a regular pattern of small s-shaped marks in the sand along the trail. But then the marks stopped and I came upon the animal that had made the marks. It was small dark-skinned eel, maybe eight inches long and thick as a man's thumb. It was lying still in the warm dry sand. But its tracks were moving in the direction of the water.

It was dead.

I picked it up in my fingers. It was what we call along the New England shoreline a black eel, smooth-skinned as a marine mammal and dead as a coffin nail. Its body had stiffened in death, so it had a kind of sine-wave configuration to it. Its eyes were still open, but vacant, and its "ears" were still sticking out from the side of its head. The ears are actually pectoral fins, I believe, but they are place so far anterior on the animal's body that they appear to be coming out of the "head."

I held the small body in my hand as I stood there. Now that I had stopped my fast pace through the sand, I was aware of the risen sun warming my dark-blue hooded sweatshirt. The day had begun for me. But not for this creature.

Now let's get one thing straight here: I'm not on any "save the eels" campaign. I've killed plenty of eels in my day in pursuit of the ever-elusive keeper striped bass. And I'll kill plenty more before I'm done. That's why my feelings that morning were a surprise to me.

I looked down again at the trail of s-shaped squiggles that had represented the animal's hopeless and doomed struggle to return to the sea.

The critter had died on the west side of a north-south road, so he was on the side of the road that vehicles coming off the beach would have taken. Back at the beginning of his struggle were the little sand craters of a loud splash of water marked in the dry sand. He had been thrown out onto the sand, probably the last eel in an bait bucket at the end of the day, and as soon as he had landed, he had begun his futile swimming along the alien sand, his skin baking in the late-afternoon sun, ambulating maybe four or five feet before his spirit left the earth.

I had feelings looking at the tracks of the dead eel. I wasn't angry or upset, just a little sad, I guess. It just seemed such a waste. Why didn't you just throw him back into the water at the end of the day? I would have asked the fisherman who dumped the bucket there.

I also felt as if I had witnessed something private; the death struggle of another living thing, a struggle that was unnecessary and useless. This wasn't just a stone or a lump of sand, it was a living animal, a clump of life, a miraculous assemblage of DNA, unique in the universe.

I made a little grave with my hiking boot, dropped the dead body there, and continued on my hike. Half an hour later, on my return trip back to where I had parked my truck, I passed the spot again. Once again I stopped. With the toe of my boot, I smoothed over the s-shaped marks of the death struggle of the eel. I knew that the wind, by the end of the day, would have done the same thing, but I just felt like I wanted to erase something.

I just wish it were as easy to erase those struggling marks from my mind.

A VERY OLD FISH TALE

As soon as I read the newspaper article in 2013, I had to write about how the same fish came into my life back in the 1960s.

The coelacanth (SEE-luh-kanth) is a primitive fish that's been in the papers this past week. Scientists have done the genome sequencing of its DNA, reported recently in the scientific journal, "Nature."

The coelacanth has long been of special interest because of the fossil record of its strange anatomy: paired lobe-like thick fatty and muscular fins that extend from its body like legs, moving in an alternating pattern, like a horse. Scientists believe these unusual fins may represent an early step - a missing link - in the evolution from fish to terrestrial four-legged animals like amphibians and reptiles, from which humans eventually evolved.

No living person had ever seen a coelacanth, presumed to have gone extinct about 65 million years ago. But then, in 1938, one came up in a fisherman's net off the African coast. Scientists were very excited; this was truly a "living fossil." They fished the area, trying to find more, and over the years, more have been caught and studied, mostly off the eastern African coast, in the Indian Ocean.

The coelacanth is a rare and elusive animal, living in waters over 2000-feet deep. An endangered species, there might be fewer than 1,000 of them on earth today. They can grow very large, over six feet long and weighing 200 lbs. Fish experts reckon that they might live to be 60 years old.

So, you might be wondering how I might be involved in a practical joke regarding a 400-million-year-old fish.

Well, back in the 1960s, I was a young man working as a commercial fisherman in Point Judith, Rhode Island, in the fishing village of Galilee, tucked into the extreme southwest corner of Narragansett Bay. In those days, the fishing community was small and tightly knit: Everyone knew each other. A few miles up the road, the University of Rhode Island had a marine biology department with a lab along the shore, and was in the process of developing a fisheries technology program. Some of the scientists and academics from the university would frequent the fishing village, doing research or fish counts or, in some cases, hanging around the waterfront pubs and socializing with the fishermen. One of these guys was Ross McDermott, a Ph.D. candidate in the marine biology program at URI.

Ross is the first of the two main characters in today's story. The second is Herb Spinney, a long-time commercial fisherman in New England waters. Herb, a high-school dropout was much more than just a fisherman. He was a man of the sea, as self-educated a man as I've met. He could discuss the history of Western Europe, the dialogues of Plato, the cooling system of a marine diesel engine, or the anatomy of a sea turtle, all with equal depth of knowledge. People around the village called Herb "The Old Dog." Ross and I were in our twenties at the time; Herb was probably in his early fifties. Ross would spend long hours engaged in conversation with Herb, either in the pub, or sitting around Herb's book-lined living room looking over the waters of Block Island Sound.

Well, one day, Herb came across an article in a science journal about the history of the coelacanth, and he took the journal on his next trip offshore - just something to peruse between watches in the wee hours of the morning. By the day he returned to shore a week later, he had digested the details of article, and knew a lot about the elusive coelacanth, which none of us had ever heard of. I believe that, on that day of Herb's return, he and Ross would have been the only guys in the fishing village to whom the word, "coelacanth" would have any meaning. And herein lies the plot of the story.

Running into Herb and me at the pub that night, Ross asked him how the trip went. Herb said, "Damndest thing happened, Ross. We brought up this giant fish in the net. At first, I thought it was a big sturgeon. But it wasn't. It was the weirdest fish I've ever seen." And then he went on to describe – in magnificent anatomical detail – the rarest of all fish on earth: the coelacanth. Ross recognized the fish from the description and was stunned as Herb went on. Finally, unable to restrain himself, he breathlessly interrupted Herb. "Where's the fish now? What did you do with it?"

"Well," Herb said without cracking a smile, "The cook cut a few steaks off it and cooked them up, but the damned meat was so oily, we couldn't eat it, so we just tossed the thing overboard."

"You tossed it overboard!" Ross exclaimed.

"Yeah," Herb said. "The big thing stunk."

Herb got up to use the head. While he was gone, Ross excitedly explained to me about the coelacanth, and that its being found in New England waters was going to rewrite a chapter in marine biology. He couldn't wait till the next morning, to tell his professors at URI. When Herb came back, he told Herb what he had told me. Herb just shrugged his shoulders.

Ross left a few minutes later. He wasn't a minute out of the door before Herb slapped me on the shoulder, started laughing and told me the truth. "You've got to tell him," I said to Herb. "He's going to tell his professors, and they'll be at your back door tomorrow."

Herb waved me away as he took another slug from his green bottle of Ballantine Ale. "You tell him," he said as he exhaled after swallowing.

A LITTLE BOY SAILS AWAY

Most parents could relate to this 2009 story of saying goodbye to a child in the midst of a time of family turmoil.

I have a standing appointment at 9 a.m. on Wednesdays with a guy I work with in Hyannis. This past Tuesday night, he called me and said he had a doctor's appointment at the hospital at 10 the next morning.

Next morning, I left messages on his phone, but got no answer, and when I got to his place, shortly after 9, he was gone – communication breakdown. Since he hadn't heard from me the night before, he may have just gone over to the hospital.

The next meeting with my fellow workers at the Duffy Health Center was at 10:15, so I had close to an hour to kill. It actually felt good.

I got a coffee at the drive-up window at Dunkin' Donuts on North Street, and headed down Ocean Street, past the fishing piers. I figured I'd go down to Kalmus Beach at the end of Ocean Street and sit in my truck, maybe correct a few philosophy exams or just listen to some music while I had my coffee and looked out in the general direction of Bermuda.

The parking lot at the beach was rippled and wavy, a sea of white snow impacted and hard. From a distance, it looked like the surface of a winter sea, and as I drove into the lot, the surface proved to be anything but smooth, like the surface of a winter sea up close would be. My truck bumped its way along, sloshing the coffee in the cup holder, until I found a break in the barrier of sand dunes and pulled into a spot looking out over the shiny dark blue water sparkling in the early March sunlight.

I punched the "ON" button on the radio and recognized

the first few bars of Beethoven's Sixth Symphony, the "Pastorale," a symphony celebrating the outdoors, the weather, and natural phenomenon. Forget those philosophy exams – I was going to sit here mindlessly with Beethoven and my coffee, the sun beating down on the cab of my black truck and warming the left shoulder of my navy-blue hooded sweatshirt as I absentmindedly stared out toward the horizon line, thinking about nothing.

And then off to my left, a flicker of motion. I turned to see the giant ferry "Martha's Vineyard" clearing the inner harbor and rounding Dunbar Point. Headed for Nantucket this morning, she rounded a harbor buoy and turned off to the southeast, setting her course.

I've been on more ferries than most people. Ferries to Block Island, to Chappaquiddick, and to many of the islands off the coast of Maine. I once got arrested on the Staten Island ferry, but that's another story for another day. I've traveled in love to Vineyard Haven and to Oak Bluffs a dozen times. Before there was a Jamestown Bridge over to Newport, and the world was young, I traveled with friends on the Newport Ferry in pursuit of the tattoo parlors on Thames Street.

Ferries from docks shaded by palm trees have delivered me to many of the islands of the Caribbean, sometimes alone, sometimes in the company of completely insane companions, sometimes with sane and sober family members, once sitting in the middle of a bunch of nuns headed for a mission church on St. John. I have ridden ferries in Northern Italy and in the Azores.

I have taken ferries from New London, Connecticut to Montauk, New York, and from Seattle to the Olympic Peninsula, as well as ferries all along Puget Sound and up among the tiny islands of the Straights of Juan de Fuca. I've bought an all-day ticket on the ferries that connect the many towns on the island of Bermuda.

But on this past Wednesday morning, I was thinking of none of these ferries. My heart was aching with bittersweet nostalgia as I watched the ferry to Nantucket move away from the shore, and I was transported to a difficult time in my life when, for a few years, I moved to Nantucket on the last day of college classes and moved back on Labor Day weekend, working on Nantucket as a stonemason, bartender, and lobster dealer.

Regularly, on many Monday mornings, I took a little twelve-year-old boy to the first ferry from Nantucket to Hyannis where his mother would be waiting for him. I'd give him his ticket, as I fidgeted unnecessarily with his backpack - anything to keep my hands on him for a few more minutes.

And then it was time. "See you next weekend!" he'd say. We'd hug and kiss and exchange "I love you"s, and then he'd trot up the ramp and quickly make his way to the stern of the upper deck, and we'd wave. Earlier in the summer, when we began this weekend ritual, he said to me, "Hey Dad, let's wave back at each other until we can't see each other any more, OK?"

I said sure, that was a good idea, and we did it.

As the boat headed for Brant Point to make its turn out into the channel, all the morning ferry traffic around the dock quickly disappeared behind me. But I'd still be there waving, a man alone, staring at a departing ferry.

Sometimes I think he could see me longer than I could see him, but not because his eyes were better than mine. Often my eyes would become blurred with the emotions that only a father can feel for a son traveling between parents on the turbulent sea of marital emotional upheaval that only adults can navigate.

So this past Wednesday, over 25 years later, I watched that

Nantucket ferry once again headed for the horizon, and damned if it didn't become blurry and disappear before it got there, just like before.

By the time I was able to blink my eyes clear again and focus on where the boat was, it was gone. Later that morning, I called my son, now a 40-year-old man, and perhaps my closest friend. I left a short message: I just told him that I was thinking about him.

AN IRISH TALE OF THE SEA

With my childhood of shiny black hair and webbed toes, this bit of old Irish folklore has stayed with me, as I explain in this 2012 column.

Early this summer I discovered a place along Nauset Beach where a small pod – two dozen or so - of gray seals regularly congregate. A long drive along the sandy beach in a 4-wheel-drive vehicle to a relatively inconspicuous spot, the seals are almost always there.

A few Mondays ago, my friend Annie and I headed out for a visit with the seals. We packed up a small cooler with cold drinks, stopped at Villa Pizza in Orleans to pick up a salad and a box containing the best pizza on Cape Cod, gassed up the Jeep at Bill's Sunoco, and headed for the sand dunes.

After our visits with the seals, Annie became quite enamored with the giant creatures. The <u>halichoerus grypus</u> are among the largest species of seals. Full-grown males are eight to eleven feet long - can weigh 900 pounds. If you knew nothing about seals and were walking along a Cape Cod beach one day as a giant male stuck only his large black head out of the water, you might think that a horse was emerging from the sea. There are horses that weigh less than a full-grown gray seal.

Loving her enthusiasm for the seals, I presented Annie with a little seal carving, handmade in Western Ireland from local granite. You'd think I had given her a 20-pound bar of solid gold. The little seal statue, long a favorite of mine, immediately disappeared. I haven't seen it since I gave it to her. I wouldn't be surprised if she sleeps with it under her pillow.

So this past Monday, we once again headed out for a visit with the seals. After driving along the sand for a while, I pulled the Jeep up to the edge of the water and shut off the engine. As if on cue, the large shiny and furry black heads with the gigantic brown eyes and long lashes, began to pop up out of the water just a few feet from the front bumper of the truck.

"She's here!" I shouted out the window to the seals, pointing to my pinnepedophiliac passenger, producing excited little girl giggles from her.

"Do you think I can go into the water with them?" she asked. I said that it would be OK. "Don't worry, they won't let you get too close," I said, answering an unasked question. "Move slowly - don't make any quick motions with your arms, and as soon as you can do so, slip down into the water so only your head is showing. That will greatly arouse their curiosity."

She stepped out onto the sand and walked slowly toward the seals. I noted that the color of her one-piece bathing suit was shiny sealskin black. Twenty-three pairs of large brown eyes were focused on her. She got to the cold water, waded in, and slowly slipped down, eye-level with the furry mammals just a few yards away.

I don't know what goes on in a seal's brain, but once the water got to her human shoulders, the seals suddenly became intensely curious, bobbing up higher in the water and moving their heads side to side to get a better look at her and focused on nothing else.

Staying motionless for long minutes in the cold Atlantic, she soon became chilled and finally emerged from the water, shivering toward the wind-sheltered warmth of the Jeep and the comfort of a sun-warmed fluffy blue towel. The seals followed her motion all the way back to the vehicle, and only turned away to their previous activity when the door slammed behind her.

"Wow," she said. "That was amazing."

"You should have seen it from here," I agreed.

Later, back at the house, I told her about my grandmother.

My grandmother O'Rourke – obviously my maternal grandparent – was a simple woman who carried many of the superstitions and rural religious beliefs of her Western Ireland heritage with her throughout her life.

One day when I was perhaps ten years old, I said to her, "My mommy (her daughter) has webbed toes."

"I know," she said laconically.

"I have webbed toes, too," I said, the only one of my mother's children to have inherited this unusual trait.

"I know," she said, tousling my shiny ink-black hair, and turning back to her kitchen work, adding over her shoulder to me: "Maybe you've both got Selkie blood." As she turned back to the stove, her body language indicated this conversation was over. I went into the front room of their little flat where my grandfather was sitting reading the paper.

I response to my question, he simply said. "A selkie? A selkie's a seal – like we see at the zoo," and returned to his paper. But I knew, even then, that there was more to this story.

I continued my story with Annie. "A few years later, I heard the word again, and found out what a selkie really was."

In Irish, Scottish and Scandinavian folklore, a selkie is a "seal woman" who emerges from the sea, shedding her skin to become human, and live as a wife and mother in a human family. Her children have shiny black hair, large eyes, small webs between their toes and an unusual affinity with the sea.

In one Celtic ballad, a seal woman lives with a fisherman and their children for many years. In bad storms at sea, he always returns safely, as he can hear her calling him from the shore, even at great distances.

One winter night, he is shipwrecked, hopelessly adrift, freezing in a winter storm. His selkie wife returns to the sea as a seal, and covers him with her warm fur, saving him from sure death. This is a major sacrifice for the selkie, for once she has returned to sea as a seal, she can never take human form again.

At the end of my account. Annie asks, "Do you really have webbed toes?" I nod my head.

Moments later, my socks are being pulled off, and we're both staring at my webbed feet.

I don't know what she's thinking, but I'm thinking about my grandmother.

The Animals

BANDIT GOES HOME

This 1998 column tells the story of my friend Jim Turner saying goodbye to a dog he had never seen.

If you had gone down to Skaket Beach in Orleans at sunset this past Thursday at dusk, just at the time of sunset, you would have found the parking lot empty except for three vehicles, all parked together in one lonely little clump, making the rest of the parking lot seem even more empty.

On the nautical almanac for this, the fifth day of March, the time of high tide in Cape Cod Bay was within an hour of sunset. The flood tide was scheduled a bit earlier than the setting of the sun, but a strong and cold easterly wind had pushed the rising Atlantic even higher into the Gulf of Maine, making the extreme tide even later, so that the two astronomical events were practically coincidental.

In the graying light of the darkening clouds, you would have seen four silent human figures out on the edge of the low-lying salt marsh, facing west, their backs to the bitter wind, hoods pulled up, hats pulled down, the icy-cold, still-rising tide lapping at their feet.

And well you might wonder what task, what calling, would bring four humans to be standing huddled at the edge of the sea on such a darkening day.

Jim Turner is a professional musician. Some years ago, he might have been called a saloon piano player. He has played around the lower end of Cape Cod for close to thirty years now. His favorite place is at the corner of a dimly-lit room, playing honky-tonk, ballads, folk, or soft rock, while people around the room, talk, eat, drink or just listen.

Jim's hands move quickly and smoothly across and around the black and white keys as he plays. His head and shoulders bob back and forth in the rhythm of the moment, and his feet rock back and forth on their heels as he works the pedals.

Not far from those feet you'd find Jim's buddy of ten years, a dog named "Bandit." Mostly black lab, but definitely cross-bred with a larger breed of some kind, the dog quickly gained a reputation around Orleans for being one of the most beautiful animals walking the streets. His massive head and broad chest might frighten those afraid of dogs, but one look from those giant brown eyes, and a lick from his massive tongue would steal the heart of anyone.

That shiny fur and gentle disposition came from years of special diet and lots of brushing and affection at the hands of Jim and his wife Nancy.

In addition to his musical talents, Jim Turner has another skill most of the rest of us, handicapped as we are, don't have. He can see in the dark just as well as he can in the bright light. This was clear a couple of years ago when he was playing down at the Barley Neck Inn in East Orleans. There was a temporary power failure while he was playing on the baby grand over in the corner of the lounge. Jim heard the murmur from the crowd and some commotion, but he just kept on playing. He doesn't use sheet music, so the lack of available light had no impact on his performance. Bandit lifted his head up for a moment, reacting to the dull confusion of the crowd, but then just put it back down on the floor, probably figuring that if Jim was continuing to play, then all must be well.

Seeing-Eye dogs are trained to be like that, cool and calm when a crisis arises.

Jim, blind from birth, remembers going down to the Seeing Eye Foundation in Morristown, NJ, in the winter of 1989, to be fitted for a dog.

"It's a complex process," Turner says. "You go down there for three weeks. They put you up in dormitory, and you live, eat and sleep there while they hook you up with a dog that fits your body size, personality, handicap, etc."

A burly guy himself, it's no surprise that the folks there fitted Turner with a burly dog. They must have also known that a creative musical artist would also be compatible with a dog who had a creative bent of his own, because that's the kind of dog Bandit turned out to be.

A couple of years ago, during a performance of "The Music Man" in Chatham, Bandit was so moved by the bass tones of the band playing the overture that he decided to join in himself. He spent the rest of the evening locked in the car outside while Jim and Nancy and a few hundred others in the audience inside enjoyed the performance with the originally scheduled cast, minus the talents of Bandit.

Jim, Nancy, and Bandit frequently stop in to the Yardarm Restaurant in Orleans for lunch. Several days ago, the three of them were there: Jim and Nancy sitting next to each other at the bar, eating, with Bandit's 125 pounds squeezed in at their feet.

The Yardarm is usually an active place at noon. Locals and fishermen frequent the place because of the prices, quality and quantity of food served there, so at lunch, many people there know each other.

But on this day, the place was a little more somber than usual. The reason for the mood change was that Bandit was the only one in the restaurant who didn't know that this day was to be his last day on earth.

About a year or so ago, he began to develop these growths on his feet, between his toes. It was very painful for him to walk. The vet removed them; Bandit recuperated. And then they started to come back, again and again. He also began to have some hip problems, maybe associated with his inability to walk properly.

The vet and Jim had the conversation. The conversation about what one does with a dog who has been not just a man's friend, but his very eyes for most of ten years.

So on this day, Bandit was going out for his last lunch. Bill North, the restaurant manager, had a special bone for him, and even gave him a little bowl of beer. Jim wasn't paying much attention to his own lunch on the bar in front of him. His left hand hung down beside him, where Bandit's upraised head provided an occasional lick to the pianist's fingers.

It is said that dogs are sensitive to the feelings of humans around them. One might wonder if Bandit was curious as to why some of the people there that day kept coming over to give him a pat, some of them unable to speak, some with tears in their eyes.

The next day, Jim Turner was walking without a dog for the first time since 1988.

Once the light began to fade from the sky, the already cold easterly wind became even more bitter than before. Nancy opened the heavy black box, pulled out the bag of crunchy gray material and handed it to Jim. The other two guys there stepped back to allow Jim and Nancy a moment alone with Bandit.

"He loved this place," Jim said softly, looking around and talking to nobody in particular.

The wind carried the ashes from Jim's hands into the tidal waters lapping at the edge of the marsh, and with each small wave, the gray remains slipped out toward the direction of the sunset, until all that was left were four humans, cold and alone in their individual thoughts.

As the quartet turned back toward the parking lot, Jim took one look back and, catching his breath, he spoke.

"Thanks, Bandit," he said. "You did a good job."

Minutes later, the parking lot was empty again; everyone had gone home.

Including Bandit.

NOT A CREATURE WAS STIRRING...

A series of winter mice visitors led me to reflect upon the relationships between animals and humans in this 1987 piece.

I live alone in a small house surrounded by woods. In the winter, if one had a mind to, the lights of other houses in this part of town could be seen by a keen observer, but, in general, my house is pretty well insulated from other human habitation. My most regularly seen neighbors are raccoons, skunks, squirrels, cats, foxes, birds of all types and, Algernon.

Algernon is the collective, generic term which I coined a few years ago for the mouse, or mice, living in the sylvan environs of my house. The name came from a wonderful play, "Flowers for Algernon," upon which the TV movie, "Charly" was based. Algernon was a pet mouse in the play.

I could set my calendar by Algernon. The first week in December brought him into the house. He would stay the winter and, come April, would disappear back into the leaves and bushes of the woods around the house. I'd see him now and then when I was in the garden or quietly working on my boat on a hot spring day, but ours has been, essentially, a winter relationship.

On cold winter nights, I would lie in bed reading, and listen to Algernon scurrying through the walls of the house. When I'm out in the living room reading or writing for long hours, I don't listen to music or TV, so my house would be as quiet as...well, as quiet as a mouse. Sometimes when I'd been working like that for a few hours, he, probably thinking that I was asleep, would venture out into the room, until he spotted me. He wouldn't retreat, but would continue to explore, with one bright brown eye on me. I liked having him around. I've never admitted this publicly before, but, on Christmas Eve, I even used to leave a cookie and a dab of peanut butter out for him. (Don't tell any of my fishing buddies about this, O.K.? They might not understand.)

So, as you can see, this relationship with Algernon has been an amicable one for a few years now. As I've said, I don't see much of him during the summer. I'm pretty busy fishing and being barefoot outdoors all summer, and he seems to be pretty busy outdoors himself during the summer months. I never knew what little brown and white mice did during the summer, but I always figured that he was pretty busy doing it, because I didn't see him much then.

This August, however, I think I got more of a notion what Algernon did over the summer. I believe that in the spring, perhaps in June, his fancy turned in the direction that the fancies of many other young males do at that time of year.

The evidence supporting my hypothesis was the increasing disarray in which I found the trash bucket under my sink in the morning. It appears that Algernon was unable to provide for his new family responsibilities by relying on the nature's bounty which had supported him during previous summers. He found it necessary to move indoors to feed his new family.

As a result of this invasion of Algernon and his dependents, on some summer mornings my kitchen was not a pretty sight. Now, nobody who knows me would describe me as a neatnick; I borrow a vacuum cleaner from a friend and vacuum the house once a year, whether it needs it or not. The dishes in the sink get done once a week, and the rain keeps my windows washed as well as need be. But things were getting out of hand. I think that the final straw was the morning I came out of the bedroom and stepped painfully barefoot on a lobster claw next to the refrigerator. That did it.

A Havahart trap is for trapping small animals, without harming them. The theory is that the animals can then be transported to another part of town where they can be released and live a happy life, away from you. For five successive days, I picked up the trap in the morning, and delivered the shivering, frightened mouse of the day to what I thought was a safe place for a mouse to live and get food. I put one in the Orleans dump (mouse heaven, right?), another next to a dumpster behind a year-round restaurant, and the other three in equally respectable mouse neighborhoods. For a week, I felt like the administrator of some federally-subsidized program for homeless mice.

That was in August, and I really haven't thought about Algernon since then. But last night I was lying in bed reading and listening to the chilly wind, and I realized that this was the first winter in years when I would not hear his scratching his way between the walls, or see his little brown body appear seemingly from nowhere, as I sat silently reading.

I put the book down on my chest, and thought about Algernon for awhile. I thought about the five mice, and I hoped that they were each snuggled in some warm furry place, with sticks and leaves, and bits of pistachio shells and sunflower seeds around them.

And I thought about the great distances that exist between us and the wild animals, and I hoped that the mice, in some primitive way, might understand that this was the way of nature, that I never meant them any harm. I realized then, how foolish it was to expect a mouse to understand how we humans in our society and way of life, are so alienated from the rest of nature, when I didn't really understand it myself, and it made me sad.

I was pulled out of my reverie by a scurrying sound along

the wall. I leaned up on one elbow and held my breath, listening for him.

But I soon realized that it was just some dead twigs blowing across the roof in the loneliness of the early December night wind.

A SHANGHAI GOODBYE

On my first trip to China, I encountered Liu Ke, a young translator who became my guide. On the day I was leaving, he gave me gift – a rhinoceros. I never hear that word without thinking of him. (2006)

RHINOCEROS (white). Noun. Massive powerful herbivorous ungulate of Africa having very thick skin and two horns on the snout.

Several years ago, I was in China on a kind of cultural exchange program between the governments of the Peoples' Republic of China and the United States.

On my first day there, I met a young man, a junior faculty member at our host college. He was to be our guide and our translator. He and I became fast friends, and spent time together outside of his official tasks.

His name was Liu Ke, Liu being his surname. Since I was older than he, it was appropriate that I call him "Chou" Liu, "chou" meaning "younger." His name for me, a kind of nickname, was "Lao-Chung-Mao." "Lao" means "older," and "chung-mao" means "panda bear."

During my time in China, it was Chou Liu's friendship that gave me a deep look into the wonderful planet called China. And it was largely because of his friendship on this first trip to China that I was inspired to apply a few years later for a Fulbright Fellowship to return to China, subsequently spending a whole summer there.

One day, we were visiting the Shanghai Zoo. There were live animals from all around the world. There were also, in a building there, a number of stuffed specimens in glassed-in displays, with painted and fabricated backgrounds, much as you would see at a museum of natural history here in America.

Chou Liu and I were alone inside a room filled with preserved specimens. The most impressive of all these was a giant stuffed white rhinoceros. I was on one side of the room, looking at some examples of small mammals native to China, and Chou Liu was across the room mesmerized by the massive rhinoceros in front of him. He had never seen one of these animals before, not even in a magazine or film, so you might imagine how a 25-year-old man might be stunned to walk into a room and find himself standing in front of one of these behemoths.

I don't know about you, but I have seen a white rhino up close; I saw one at a zoo in Florida last year. They can grow to be six feet tall, and weigh up to 8000 pounds –the weight of two pickup trucks! The only larger terrestrial animal is the elephant. And although they are pure vegetarians, rhinos are still very dangerous to humans, responsible for more deaths than lions and tigers combined. They have even been known to attack elephants. This maybe explained by the fact that rhinos have notoriously bad eyesight.

In any case, the display at the Shanghai Zoo was elevated a couple of feet off the floor of the display room, so this gargantuan example of the taxidermist's skills looked to be the size of a gray trailer truck in a glass case. I can only imagine what it looked like to the five-foot-tall, 125-lb. Mr. Liu.

He called softly to me from across the room. "Lao-Chung-Mao!" I turned to look his way. The rhinoceros was big, but I'd seen dozens of pictures, films and real live rhinoceroses in my lifetime, so I was more interested in the fauna of China, including some very interesting little critters I had never seen before.

He was beckoning me to come to where he was. He didn't move his feet, and his head was just slightly turned my way, as if trying to keep one eye on the rhinoceros, lest it disappear should he let it out of his sight.

As I looked across the room, I was struck by how tiny he looked against the elevated display of the giant primitive-looking animal. He looked smaller than he was, and the rhino looked larger than it was in some kind of simple optical illusion.

I crossed the room and stood next to him. He was still wide-eyed. He pointed to the plaque on the base of the display. There were some Chinese words there. "Lao-Chung-Mao," he said to me, "How do you say the name of this animal in English?"

Now, Liu spoke perfect English, with a decided accent to be sure, but grammatically perfect. I pronounced the word "rhinoceros" slowly for him. He repeated it for me slowly, and it was hard not to laugh. You would never recognize what he was trying to say.

I went over the etymology of the word for him, explaining that it came directly from two Greek words, "rhino" which means "nose" and "ceros" which means "horn." He repeated the word again, but he definitely was not getting the pronunciation. It was like he had some kind of mental block about the syllables.

As the summer went by, we joked about the word, and now and then I would just spontaneously utter the word out loud. This could happen on a bus, while having lunch, or maybe just walking across campus. As soon as I said it, he would repeat his version of the noun identifying the large African mammal, and I would purse my lips and shake my head at his failure, then we'd both laugh.

On my last day in Shanghai, he insisted on coming to the airport to see me off. At dinner the night before he said he had "two gifts" for me. At the airport, things went fast, and we were soon saying goodbye at the security area. I gave him a big panda bear hug, and he handed me a tiny brass Buddha. It is one of my most precious possessions. I'm looking at it as I write these words.

We were both struggling to hold back tears, but were succeeding. I turned my back and headed for the gate. I had only taken four or five steps when from behind me, I heard a voice calling, "Lao-Chung-Mao!"

I turned and looked into the big smiling face of this tiny man, my first true Chinese friend. He had one index finger pointing into the air. He licked his lips, took a deep breath, and spoke a word. Just one word. It was perfect. He must have been up all night practicing. "Rye-NAH-sir-us!" he said, with a big exaggerated accent on the second syllable much as young child might do. I was struck silent, and in that silence, he said it again, really sounding like a kindergartner this time: "Rye-NAH-sir-us!"

I not sure whether I was laughing or crying, probably both, but our eyes met in a powerful and silent communication, I nodded my head vigorously, for I could not speak, then I turned back toward the plane, my eyes blurred with tears, and began to move down the ramp.

And in that instant, Chou Liu's second gift, those four syllables, perfectly and slowly pronounced, entered my ears and took root in my heart, where they remain to this day.

A CHIPMUNK LEAVES MASSACHUSETTS

An encounter with a tiny animal in the great woods of Western Massachusetts provided me with an intense and unexpected spiritual experience. (2006)

My brother Tom and I have occasionally sparred about the relative greatness of our favorite classical music composers. He speaks for Beethoven; I for Mozart.

Several years ago, we were sitting at my kitchen table discussing pieces of music, perhaps listening to same, when, in an attempt to elevate my guy over his guy, I pointed out to him that Mozart had written over 40 symphonies. His quick retort was, "Perhaps, but he never wrote a 'Ninth,'" referring, of course, to the famous Ninth Symphony of Beethoven, the so-called "choral" symphony.

It was true: Mozart had written over 40 symphonies, and Beethoven had written only nine, and yet.... I looked across the table at my brother, sitting there looking like a chess player who had just moved his knight into a checkmate position against his opponent's king and was waiting for the opponent to realize what had happened. He knew he had me. I nodded my head slowly, smiled back at him and said, "You're right."

Even a Mozart worshipper such as I must admit that nobody has ever written a piece of music to compare with Beethoven's Ninth. The fourth and final movement contains the famous "Ode to Joy" based on a piece by the great German poet Friedrich Schiller. Few music lovers have ever seen the Ninth Symphony done live. Fewer have seen it done live by a world-class symphony orchestra such as the Boston Symphony Orchestra. And I'll tell you, there are not many who have ever seen Beethoven's Ninth done at Tanglewood, the summer home of the BSO, featuring the performance of the Tanglewood Festival Chorus.

So when I saw the summer schedule for Tanglewood posted this past spring, I moved quickly to the phone and dialed and redialed until I was able to secure two seats for opening night in July, and a performance of the Ninth. Joseph Levine, musical director of the BSO and immediate successor of Seiji Ozawa, had been injured earlier in the year in a fall and had not been conducting. He was expected to make his debut return on that night, adding to the drama of the Friday evening production. I heard later that all seats had sold out in 48 hours.

I picked up my friend Kate in Amherst on Thursday; we got back on the Mass Pike and went to Exit 1, the last exit on the Pike at West Stockbridge. Five minutes later, we were at the home of Peggy Rae, Howie and Sierra Wilson, in the wooded little town of Alford hidden away in the Berkshire hills above Great Barrington, a wandering black bear's day trip from the New York State border, just over the mountain.

Peggy Rae and Howie are dear old friends. She was my student at CCCC many years ago. I was the homilist at their wedding in Alford back in the late 1980s. Their daughter Sierra is my godchild. Kate had not met them before, but three minutes with the Wilsons and you're family - once you're accepted by their dog Romeo who protects the dozens of chickens, turkeys and other animals that call this place home.

We had a delicious dinner, replete with home-grown vegetables and wonderful conversation, but it had been a long day for all of us, and we all turned in early. On Friday morning, the house was quiet, as Howie and Peggy were off to work and Sierra was at camp. We decided that we would do some exploring.

Kate wanted to take a drive over to Jacob's Pillow, the world-famous dance center in the neighboring town of Becket. She was interested in applying for work there. I waited in the truck, reading, while she went into the office and did some business.

By the time she returned, the sun was getting lower in the sky, and it was time that we headed back to Howie and Peggy's to change and get ready for the concert at Tanglewood that night.

At the bottom of the hill coming down from Jacob's Pillow, a car quickly turned into the road we were on, and as it passed, it ran over a small animal in the road. I did not see this happen, but Kate did. She let out a tiny scream, as I brought the truck to a stop at the intersection with the main highway. From the truck we could look back and see the small animal writhing in pain and making tiny noises.

We talked quietly for a minute. Then I put on the flashing hazard light on my truck, got out, and walked back to where the animal was lying in the road. It was a chipmunk. It appeared to have suffered a broken back, as the top part of its body seemed to be functioning, its front paws trying to run, but the lower extremities were limp and lifeless. Its eyes were open and its mouth was making unpleasant sounds.

I stood there for a moment, looking at the agony of the tiny creature at my feet, looking at the beauty of the Berkshire forest around me, breathing the beautiful oxygenated air of the hills here. I knew what I had to do. It wasn't as if I had any humane choice. I just wanted to try to do it gently, if there is any such thing.

For just a few seconds, I heard and saw nothing in the world around me, so intense was my concentration on the task before me. My encounter with death was intimate and engaging; I was a part of it. I squatted down next to the unfortunate animal, and did what needed to be done. And as I arose, and the soul of the chipmunk rose with me, a part of me went a short way with it, then stopped, as the chipmunk soul continued on its journey. The first thing I heard when I returned to Massachusetts was the idling of my truck engine behind me.

Later that night at Tanglewood, the voices of close to 200 singers and perhaps 100 musicians finished the vigorous fourth movement of Beethoven's Ninth, and every person in attendance was standing and applauding for several encores, the "Ode to Joy" still echoing in our consciousness. After the concert, a magnificent fireworks display followed for long minutes, and the joyful crowd out on the expansive lawn "oohed" and "aahed" with each explosion high in the sky.

Lying in bed later that night, I reflected upon the Tibetan Buddhist assertion that in order to experience joy in life, we must encounter death and come to integrate it, to realize it into our consciousness of life. I believe this. And I also believe that, on some days, we can come a little bit closer to this realization than on others.

CODY THE DOG SAYS HIS GOODBYES

My brother Richard is a dog lover, as am I. He often spoke of Cody, a dog who lived on their long dead-end street in a mountain valley in Western Washington state. Cody, and the McCullough family dog, Ringo, were best buddies. When Richard called and told me this story in 2002, I knew I had to write it.

Sixty miles east of Seattle, the 8,000-ft. snow-covered peak of Mt. Daniel lies among a throng of its frozen and barren sisters in the breathtakingly beautiful Cascade Mountains of Western Washington State. The Snoqualime River rises there and flows west toward the Pacific.

About halfway along that trip, the Snoqualmie River runs through the small city of North Bend – 30 miles or so east of Seattle, the river bends slowly to the north – hence the name of the town - and runs out of land 50 miles later at the Tulalip Indian Reservation up on Puget Sound.

North Bend itself is a sleepy little town, strikingly beautiful for the snow-covered mountains surrounding the valley in which it lies. I-90, which begins somewhere down around the Prudential Tower in Boston, runs through North Bend just before it ends in Seattle.

A long residential street, S.E. Tanner Road, runs a mile or so out from I-90 and dead-ends at the river. When the water is low, before the spring runoff from the mountains, the river "talks" as it gurgles and plucks its musical way among the rocky river bottom.

Cody the dog lived on S.E. Tanner Road, among the tall trees there. Not tall by West Coast standards, to be sure, but massive and impressive by New England measurements. There's might be a tree on that road that's taller than any tree in New England.

Cody was a big dog, maybe a cross between a long-haired German Shepherd and a large Golden Retriever. My brother Richard, who lives on the street, described him this past Thursday as we talked. "He was like one of those big dogs that you see in kid's movies where they want to have a great big loveable dog playing around with the kids. That was Cody," he told me.

Cody had a ritual every morning and night. His master, a single guy who lived halfway down the road, would feed him and then let him out for his walk. Cody would be on his own, no leash, just a big guy out for his morning or evening constitutional, unaccompanied by his master. He'd wander along the street, first down one side on his way out, and then, getting to the cul-de-sac at the end of the road where Richard lives, he'd stop and turn back for home, traveling along the opposite and yet unvisited side of the street.

At this point, he'd make a special stop to sniff around and visit at Rich's house for a few minutes with his buddy, Ringo. Richard and his family had a beloved Corgi hound who was like a member of the family. Unlike his buddy Cody, Ringo was not a wanderer, and would tend to stay close to home, but he'd be up for some socializing twice a day when his friend Cody showed up.

Everyone on the road knew Cody. If dogs had elected officials, Cody would be the canine mayor of the Snoqualmie Valley, or at least the part of the valley described by S.E. Tanner Road. His making his twice daily rounds, performing the canine equivalent of shaking hands, kissing babies, and saying, "Nice t' see ya'" to each of his constituents.

There was a joke among the folks along the road. That was that Cody could actually smile. "I know it sounds crazy," Richard said to me," But he had this little curl around his lip; you had to see it." When people would greet the loveable

Cody with doggie talk like, "Oooh Cody boy, good boy, good boy," and rub his head, he'd look up and the side of his lip would pull back in a little curl. It was impossible not to laugh at his appearance at that point, and of course, Cody thought it was all about him, and would bask in the attention.

When Rich's own dog, Ringo, died in 1997, Rich and his family were devastated. His two sons had grown up with Ringo, and the family loved the dog as one of its own. One of the saddest sequels to Ringo's departure would now and then occur at suppertime.

Winter nights come early in the day to mountain valleys. S.E. Tanner way was often shrouded in darkness by dinner. The family would be eating at the dining room table, when one of them would have the feeling that someone was watching. And there, out behind the sliding doors on the deck overlooking the river, would be Cody, staring silently into the lighted house.

He wasn't looking for food; he had just had his dinner. The family knew what he was looking for, and the realization could bring tears to any one of the four of them sitting there staring silently back at the patient Cody, waiting for his buddy Ringo to appear.

Well, Cody continued his rounds of the neighborhood as the years went by, and by last year, he himself was in his 15th year of life, having spent almost a dozen of those years on this road. His step was a little less sure, his gait not as steady, but like the senior ambassador without portfolio that he was, he continued with dignity and an attitude of "This is a tough job – walking this neighborhood, but someone's got to do it."

Then one day, Cody appeared on his late afternoon rounds accompanied by his master, a man Rich had never even met before. The day was unusual insofar as Cody never made his rounds with his master. Cody had failed in a noticeable way. As he made his way along the road, his back legs would shudder a little and his rear end would involuntarily settle to the ground. His master would walk back, take him gently by the hips, put him back on his feet, and Cody would continue his rounds. The human master had become the valet, tending to the real canine master of this neighborhood.

On this day, occasionally Cody would voluntarily just stop and sit in place, as if taking a break. His master made no move to help him; Cody was looking up at him as if to say "I'm OK; I just need to stop for a minute." The man would just wait until Cody was ready. Then he'd struggle to his feet and continue his rounds.

When they got to Rich's house, Rich was out in his front yard. He approached Cody and his master. The man shook hands with Richard, introduced himself, and began to speak.

"Cody's come to say goodbye to all his friends," he said. As Rich looked at the man's face, he could see he had been crying. Rich himself could hardly speak.

The man began weeping, and rambled on, almost talking to himself. "They say he's suffering; they say I've got to put him away. I just can't do it. But I've got to do it, don't I? We've got an appointment for tomorrow."

Rich doesn't remember much of the rest of the conversation, but he remembers watching Cody and his master slowly continue their painful rounds back up the other side of the street. He watched the man stop at houses, and introduce himself to strangers, Cody's friends. And then they were gone. "I never saw them again," Rich says.

But I'd like to think that on some early winter night, a neighbor coming home from work might, just for a second, out of the corner of his eye, see a flash of tan and black fur along the side of the road, then look again and find nothing there.

And I'd like to think that neighbor might remember that once there was a gentle and loving being who came down this street to say hello every day, bringing his own special smile with him.

TIMMY TAKES A WALK DOWNTOWN

Tacked on the front of my refrigerator, I still have a picture of Timmy, the main character in this warm story that came to me on a very cold winter day in 1995.

The first time I met Timmy he was walking down Main Street in East Orleans, not far from the Academy of Performing Arts opposite Monument Road.

I really couldn't help notice him, since he was walking down the middle of the road, right on the double yellow line. It was about 11 o'clock in the morning, and I remember that it was a bright sunny winter day, a day or two before Christmas.

He looked as if he were headed for town. Most of the cars and trucks that swerved around him as they passed were headed for town too, folks on their lunch hours going downtown to run errands or maybe just people going into Orleans Village Center to do some last minute Christmas shopping.

He didn't seem to notice the traffic very much he was just trudging along at a casual pace eyes downcast, looking at the double yellow line as if he were a bloodhound. But he wasn't a bloodhound; he was a golden retriever.

I pulled my truck over, jumped out, and worked my out to the yellow line, following the dog. I called to him, but he didn't answer. I shouted loudly at him; he didn't even twitch his ears, but just kept moving along head down following the double yellow line. It occurred to me that he might be deaf.

I was wearing a big knitted cap that has a high peak going straight up, a large bulky sweater and some old painter's pants. Although it was cold out, I had on my feet a pair of sandals with no socks. I was out running a quick errand, and I hadn't expected to have to leave my truck for more than a minute. My toes were measuring the chill.

As I kept calling to him and following the yellow line with him, I fantasized that it wouldn't be a surprise to the motorists swerving and passing a few feet either side of us if a lion, a tin man, and a scarecrow were marching along with us, along the yellow-marked road.

I finally caught up with the dog, took his collar in hand, and managed to escort him over to the side of the road. I knelt down next to him and, murmuring encouraging words, slipped my fingers under the collar to see if he had any identification. I didn't have to look any further. The collar itself was embroidered with the five-letter word, "TIMMY," and a seven-digit Orleans telephone number.

I put my hand under his grey face, which contrasted with his golden body. His beard was the same color as mine. I tilted his face up to mine and looked into the giant brown eyes.

"Well Timmy, we've got to get you home, don't we?" His tail wagged at the mention of the two syllables printed on the collar. I got him into my truck and turned the heater on. In 30 seconds, he was asleep on the floor of the passenger's compartment, his face up against the heater outlet there.

I called the number on the collar, and a short while later, I was dropping him at his home. I had assumed, because of his advanced years (I found out later that he was 16 years old), that he must have lived within a few hundred yards of where I found him. Wrong.

The house was about five miles away. His owner, Jim Rogers, was a man in his late eighties, maybe early nineties, and still played tennis a couple of times a week. Rogers said of Timmy, "Yup, he likes to take those long walks into town." These two belonged together, I thought to myself. These two really belong together.

Close to a year later, I learned that they were not together any more. One day, a woman approached me in Orleans, identified herself as Caroline Hill, and asked me if I remembered Timmy the dog.

I laughed a little. "Of course; of course. How's he doing?"

"Well," she said, "I guess he's doing OK, but Mr. Rogers, his master, died recently and we're trying to find a home for Timmy."

The problem was that nobody wants a 17-year-old dog, even a healthy, handsome specimen like Timmy. This week, someone who knows a lot about dogs told me those years in a dog are equivalent in human terms to 120 years of age. To take a dog like that to the Animal Rescue League would not be fair or humane.

Caroline looked up at me and I shook my head for two reasons. First, in sadness for old Timmy to have lost his best friend, and second, shaking her head in response to the question I knew she was going to ask me.

Well, I talked to Caroline Hill again a few days later. All is well, thanks to some special humans who guided Timmy to a safe place after his lifetime best friend just disappeared one day. It seems that Richard Birmingham, a caretaker at Jim Rogers' house, had been riding around town in his 1963 Mercury convertible with Timmy riding shotgun. Taped to the car was a cardboard sign which said, in essence, "OLD DOG NEEDS NEW HOME."

In the little Windmill Plaza Shopping Center, by the East Orleans Post Office, there is a neat little gift and card shop, called "Nory's." Nory herself noticed the young guy, the dog, the car, the sign. She knew Caroline Hill; knew that Caroline was involved in a Golden Retriever organization.

Hill knew a woman named Joan Dalburg who was

involved in the same organization. They talked. Joan asked about Timmy, got some details about his health. She met him, sort of an interview, I guess, and Timmy got a home: Joan Dalburg's home. She has a six-year-old Golden Retriever named "Rocket." I talked to her this week. "How's Timmy doing?" I asked.

"Oh, he's doing fine," she said. "He's right here with me now, while I'm talking to you." She told me she was walking the dogs along Skaket Beach the other day. Another woman was walking a big mastiff. In a friendly way, the mastiff wandered over to check out Rocket, Timmy and Joan. Timmy gave him a big growl. "He doesn't know he's sixteen," she said.

When Jim Roger's heirs transferred guardianship of Timmy over to Joan Dalberg, they included papers authorizing her to have Timmy euthanized if he should become so sick or feeble that it would be humane to do so. Sort of a living will. "When that happens," she told me, "I'm going to have him cremated and spread his ashes over Jim Rogers' grave."

Later, I thought about Timmy and Jim, back together again. And I thought of how often animals bring out the best in us.

RASCAL THE CROW GOES TO SEA

It's amazing how truth can be funnier and stranger than fiction. This story of a conversation I had with an Orleans lobsterman, my friend Mike Kartasiewicz, in 1994 is a perfect example of a story that cried out to be told.

The guys who fish for a living out of Nauset Harbor in Orleans are not just fishermen, they're seamen as well. Every time they go out they need to cross the bar at Nauset Inlet, one of the most treacherous passages of water on the East Coast. The inlet cannot be navigated at low tide, because of the exposed sandbars, so these guys are forced to live their live according to the tide tables.

If they are lucky with the weather, wind and tide, they can skillfully slide out into the open ocean and go fishing. That's the easy part - getting out. Then, a dozen hours later, they need to reverse the process as they come back in again, hopefully with a load of lobster or groundfish.

Getting back in is always trickier than going out. A following sea is always more dangerous than one on your bow. And once your stern gets pushed a little bit to the side in the surf piling up behind you coming through Nauset Inlet, you're done for.

I know. I've come in and out of the inlet 100 times. And it's never the same. Each trip is a different experience. Sometimes it's like skimming across a mill pond in some quiet English village. You could have a cup of tea on the seat next to you, and never spill a drop. Other days, it's like standing up in the front car of a roller coaster while firefighters spray high-pressure hoses in your face, tearing your hat off your head and blowing your cheap sunglasses into the surf behind you.

On days like this, the first thing to be done once your safely across the bar and into the harbor is stop for a minute to put your tools back into the toolbox that has crashed and exploded all over the deck, and pick up all the fishing gear and clothing strewn around the boat. If you've lived on Cape Cod for more than a week, you know how the weather, and the seas, can change in 12 hours. If, while these guys are out fishing, the weather turns sour, they have to head for home.

The ocean East of Cape Cod is called by many "The Graveyard of the Atlantic," because of the hundreds of ships that have come to their final end on the shallow bars just offshore along either side of Nauset Inlet. Faced between sitting out there in a nasty storm or braving the gauntlet of surf at the inlet, the choice is not pretty, but it's clear: you have to come in.

Mike Kartasiewicz is one of the guys who makes his living going in and out of Nauset Inlet. His big lobster boat, the "Loon Cry," can be seen almost every day coming in and out as he tends his hundreds of lobster pots in the offshore waters.

Mike is wiry and lean guy with a very low percentage of body fat. There are no chubby guys working commercial fishing boats out of Nauset Harbor. Although he's not that old, he has a shock of white hair sticking out of his salty old baseball cap. I've known him for 30 years. His hair has been white all that time. I think he must have had white hair when he was a kid.

Mike is a bachelor. He does his own laundry, doesn't shave every day and he likes to smoke cigars, so if you were standing around the shore watching the boats come in, and Mike pulled up and jumped out of his beat-up pickup truck, he could appear to be a pretty tough-looking guy. When he's got a cigar in his mouth, he talks a little bit out of the side of his mouth, adding to the Popeye image.

But underneath it all, he's one nice guy. He has a great sense of humor, a generous spirit, and a friendly way about him once you get to know him. He is a gentleman when ladies are present and loves to talk. He's one of those guys I never pass with just a "hello." If our trucks wind up side-by-side in the parking lot down at the harbor, I always roll down my window to chat. Same around town, at the Stop & Shop or the Post Office: if I see Mike, we always stop for at least a minute.

A few days ago, on Thursday of this past week, I was talking to Dave Bessom, an Orleans native who has fished and run boats on the Outer Cape for 30 years. He and Mike are good buddies. We got talking about Mike. I asked him what Mike was up to; I hadn't seen him in a few weeks.

"You better check in with him," Dave said. "He's kind of down." He went on to say that Mike had suffered a loss recently.

I chased Mike down a little later.

"How's it goin'," I asked.

"Ah, Dan," Mike growled in his foghorn voice, "The damn cat next door ate my pet crow."

"Oh, jeez, I'm sorry Mike. When did it happen?"

"Just a couple of days ago. It's awful."

"Yeah, yeah," I commiserated. "So how long did you have the crow?"

Mike explained that he was out in his yard in East Orleans sometime after Fourth of July and heard a big commotion in the trees out back. When he investigated he found a young crow on the ground, unable to fly. No broken bones or other injuries, but his tail feathers looked a little weird, and he couldn't fly.

Mike took him in. Fed him. The crow adopted Mike.

Figured he was his mother or something. I've read where birds do that. Mike named him "Rascal." The crow would chase balls across the floor and retrieve them. Same with rubber bands, Mike told me.

"I took him out fishing with me one day," Mike told me.

"You did not!" I said laughing.

"No, no. I did."

"How did he like it?" I asked.

"Well, OK, I guess."

Like I've said, I've known Mike a long time; I knew there was more to this boat story, so I just stood there and waited for Mike to resume the conversation.

"They gave good weather in the morning, so I figured it'd be a good day to break him in offshore, you know?"

"Yeah, sure," I said, nodding my head as if it made perfectly good sense to take a pet crow out on the North Atlantic.

Mike continued: "Well I'll be damned if it didn't come up easterly and blow hard. It was nasty out there. Crazy how that weather can change like that."

"How did Rascal do?"

"Oh, he wasn't that happy with the whole thing. Like I said it was pretty rough. But he sat down on the bunk and kept his sea legs. He looked like he might have been a little seasick, but he was OK. You think crows can get seasick, Dan?"

I just shrugged my shoulders as if he had asked me a question about theoretical sub-atomic physics.

"I really miss him," Mike said. "Now I really know how people feel when they lose a pet."

"Yeah," I said. "It's tough."

"We used to watch TV at night. You know, just for an hour or so. He'd get tired by about nine o'clock. Then I'd put him to bed. I made a little roost for him out in the garage."

"Watch TV?" I asked, my eyebrows arching up into my

forehead.

"Yeah. He liked the TV. After the bad experience with boat, you know, he didn't want to go fishing anymore. He'd mostly just stay at home and watch TV."

I swallowed hard, trying not to crack up, aware of the bizarre conversation I was in. But, with straight face, I had to ask. "Did he, uh, like, have a favorite show or anything?"

"Yeah," Mike said seriously. "His favorite was the Weather Channel."

I didn't say a word. I didn't even smile.

I just nodded my head.

The Dead

GOODBYE AND THANKS TO MY FATHER

I wrote this column the day after my father died in 1988, even before his funeral. Within a week, I got over 100 pieces of mail - mostly from men. Other men called me on the phone and wept openly for what they <u>didn't</u> have with their fathers.

Those of you who read obituaries in this newspaper may have also noticed a familiar name – my name – on those pages a few days ago. The dead man was my father; he gave me his name at birth. I'm a junior. He died on Monday, six days ago.

I want to tell you today a little bit about the old man and myself. I believe that it isn't just an issue of one father and one son. I think that the relationship between us makes a universal statement.

When I was a boy, growing up in the inner city of Providence, we were poor. We didn't know that we were poor, but we were. Often Christmas and Thanksgiving turkeys came from the church or from thoughtful neighbors.

There were occasionally holidays when more than one turkey arrived. Some years, with Thanksgiving and Christmas so close together, the turkey menu at the little inner-city bungalow in which the nine of us lived strained even my mother's creative culinary imagination. Even a woman who could make creamed codfish every Friday night taste good was challenged by two months of turkey.

I was often glad to see January, and shuddered at the possibility that there was a January holiday which might inspire the benevolent to distribute more turkeys to us poor folks.

In the world in which I grew up, each child in the family was expected to make some significant contribution to the maintenance of the household. One of my sisters worked as a governess to make money to help out. Others were more comfortable staying at home and helping with domestic chores, etc. One brother worked at a gas station. Another brother was a sensitive and caring young man intelligent and competent to take care of our youngest brother, a special needs baby. As the oldest, I felt good about going out into the world of working men and then giving my parents the money I had earned. This sense of family participation was ingrained in us. As the oldest in the family, I was especially sensitive to it.

When I was about twenty, I was beginning to plan my own life. I had pretty much decided that to be a commercial fisherman, and was planning to move out of the house to pursue that goal. I knew that I would be the first to leave the nest, and I was concerned about the financial gap created by my departure.

It wasn't that any of us was such a great support to the family; my father had always worked three, and often four, jobs. (There was a period in my life when I thought that any of my schoolmates' dads who worked only two jobs must have been physically disabled, or just plain lazy.) But the cumulative effect of each of the adolescent children chipping in a little bit was significant.

I felt uncomfortable with the prospect of leaving the family; I spoke to my father, and told him this. We were alone in my small room in the cellar of the house. He put a hand on my arm and said words to me which I've never forgotten. He said to me, "You didn't ask to be born; your mother and I brought you and your brothers and sisters into this world. You have made our lives better. Go and do what you need to do.

You owe us nothing."

In those few words, he set me free - free from the manipulation, interference, and meddling that I have seen so many children receive at the hands of parents (all done in the name of love, of course). I cannot count the number of times those words have come back to me. They have been a source of liberation to me all of my life.

When my son was getting ready to leave for college a few years ago, I told him the same thing; I also told him where I had first heard the words. If he has a child someday, perhaps he'll do the same.

Twenty years after my father spoke the above words to me, he and I were out walking on the Brewster clam flats. It was a beautiful early summer day: no tourists, no wind, plenty of sunshine and a low tide.

My father was in his early seventies at the time. I had slowly begun to realize that he was not immortal. We trudged barefoot between the sandbars, through the small channels warmed by the sun. The warm salt water shallows were teeming life: small crabs and stranded minnows, waiting for the return of the tide.

As we walked, we spoke of death. I told him of my fears and my experiences. He told me of his. We talked on and on, and we walked further than we should have. His feet were tired, he said. I hadn't realized how far out on the dimensionless tidal flats we had walked, but when father and son are speaking openly and passionately of death, time and distance are forgotten.

We turned and began the long walk back to where we had parked. We walked in silence. After a long conversation about death, there wasn't much to say. Somewhere along the way back, I stopped him. I put both my hands on his shoulders, looked him in the eyes and told him that when he died, I would cry. But I told him that I would not shed one tear because there was something left unsaid between us. And I told him that I loved him so very much for that.

I held his still-warm body in my arms this week and I wept. I held my mother, my sisters, my brothers in my arms this week, and I wept. I stood at the cemetery this past Friday, forty-eight hours ago, and I wept. Tears in my eyes blur my typing as I write these words.

But I remember our walk on the Brewster clam flats, and I know that I haven't shed a tear this week because there was any unfinished business between us.

Thanks, Pop.

VISITING THE FISH AND A FRIEND

I wrote this 1988 column a year after my friend Ernie Gage died. I will never go back to the spring run of herring in Brewster without thinking of him.

I did something this week which I have done every year at this time for close to 20 years: I went to the Brewster herring run on Stony Brook Road.

It's a warm May day, and I'm walking the path which runs along Stony Brook, at the herring run. Stony Brook Valley, which cradles the Brook from Lower Mill Pond to Cape Cod Bay, is shady, dark and cool. It is late afternoon, and I can still see the sun on the pregnant treetops of the tall trees bordering the Valley. The afternoon crowds are gone, and I'm alone with the chuckling brook, the herring, and my thoughts.

I can recall when I first moved to Brewster and bought a house a half mile from where I'm standing, on Stony Brook Road. It was a short walk down to "the run", and, in the spring, each of the neighbors would hope to be the first to see an alewife swimming its relentless way upstream to Lower Mill Pond and beyond.

I remember going to the mouth of the run, at Paine's Creek Beach, at midnight one clear moonlit night, and watching the speechless clamoring of the thousands of silver bodies struggling to get to their upstream destiny. My reporting the wonder of this nocturnal experience to my ten-year old son later that day soon elicited a sworn paternal promise to bring him there the next night – if he followed his mother's dictum that he go to bed especially early.

I awakened him as promised, and by 2 AM, we were on our bicycles, coasting down to the beach to watch. The show was as spectacular as the night before, actually more so; the moon had waxed in the preceding 24 hours, and was practically overhead by the time we got there. It was like daylight. We watched quietly and reverently. Later, I remember lying on our backs on the cool April sand, each thinking private thoughts, father and son. I remember the face of a little boy in the moonlight. Oh, yes, I remember that night well, for a lot of reasons.

I have gone to the herring run other Aprils and Mays, alone, when things in my life were not as I would have them be, and have found solace in the order and stability which the run presented to my chaotic state of mind.

And I have watched sunsets at the mouth of the run with a dear friend, and wrote musical notes in the sand, with our toes. The music has long since been washed away, of course. The friendship endures.

So I'm back at the run this week. Although the memories above are with me this year, there is one overwhelming presence for me in this May of 1988. I'm thinking of my friend and neighbor, Ernest Gage, who lived on the top of the hill opposite the old mill at the herring run. Ernie was one of those rarities these days: a native Cape Codder. His family has been in Brewster for generations. Most of his brothers and sisters still live in Brewster, as do many nieces and nephews, and his widow, Rosamund.

Back around 1970, my friend, Bert Malatesta, and I both moved to Brewster within a year or so of each other. Bert was here first. He was into organic gardening and farming at the time, so it was inevitable that he would run into Ernie Gage. It may be hard for some to imagine, but in those days, circa 1970, you could drive from one end of Brewster to the other and meet half the population driving on Route 6A.

When I got to town, Bert was quick to introduce me

to Ernie. We hit it off instantly. He was a farmer (actually, THE farmer, at the Barnstable County Farm, for 30 years), a beekeeper, a dog breeder, cat lover, gardener par excellence, and had forgotten more about the history of Brewster than most people in town remembered. When someone had a problem or question on anything from tomato plants to a sick dog, or the history of an old road in town, the response in the neighborhood was always, "Call Ernie!" He'd stop by the house, look at the problem, recognize it with a smile and give the necessary advice and/or help needed. He was a good neighbor, in the fullest sense of the word.

Ernie was the first person I met in my life who loved a town. He loved a town. He loved Brewster, and Brewster and its inhabitants were the better for it. He lived here all his life. Just think of that - how many persons reading these words this Sunday have lived in the same town for a lifetime? It's unheard of today. It's practically un-American.

Over a 20-year period, he was on several town boards and committees. When zoning first came to town, many locals were wary and suspicious. Ernie had the foresight to see what Brewster might look like 20 years ahead, and was active, with his wife, Roz, in seeing that Brewster grew in a healthy way. As I said, he loved this town.

There were many people who didn't agree with the way that Ernie thought about some subjects, but I didn't know anyone who disliked him. He was opinionated and, if asked, would tell you exactly how he felt on any subject. He wasn't much of a diplomat. He had no use for lawyers, fast-talking land developers, "city slickers," or Democrats. One year, some teenagers I know (who will today remain nameless) put a "Studds for Congress" bumper sticker on Ernie's truck. (Studds was an openly gay Democrat) He drove around with it for a few days, and wasn't smiling when he discovered it.

If Ernie's love in general was the Town of Brewster, his love in particular was the Stony Brook Herring Run. It is for that reason that I feel his presence here today. He was chairman of the Alewife Committee for over a dozen years. The years that he was not actually on the Committee, he was certainly there ex officio; few people in town, with possible exceptions such as John Hay and Harry Alexander, knew more about the herring than did Ernie. He taught me the mystery and magic of the herring, and I taught my son the same.

As the herring do each year, Ernie found his way upstream to his final destination last spring. I believe this would have been the first time that he had not been to Stony Brook for the spring run since the day he was born, 64 years ago.

So, Ernie, I'm here to report today that the herring are running again. And, although you don't walk here any more, all is well; the annual cycle here is once again in motion. Things continue without you, and I know that's O.K. with you.

American Indians say that as long as a dead man is remembered, his spirit stays alive. So, I'm not feeling so alone here with the herring, after all.

A FRIEND LOST AT SEA

Herbie Spinney was one of my closest friends during the years I was a commercial fisherman in Point Judith, Rhode Island. When we heard how he died, we all said, "Of course." I wrote this column in 1988.

My first social encounter with Herb Spinney occurred about 75 miles offshore. We were fishing the edge of the continental shelf, south of Nantucket Island.

I was working out of Point Judith, R.I. on a big eastern-rigged Gamage trawler. Our boat was hauled out for repairs, so our crew was out of work temporarily. The married guys used the unexpected sabbatical to reacquaint themselves with their wives and kids, get the garage cleaned out, or the house painted. I looked for a week's work.

I asked around the fishing village, and found some work. I signed on for a "transit trip" on a boat with a captain and crew who were all strangers to me. A "transit trip", in fishing lingo, is a job that a fisherman takes for one trip only. It usually occurs, as it did in my case, when a crewmember is hurt, or takes a trip off for some reason. The captain hires someone to take the crewmember's place for that one trip. I was that guy. Herb was the captain.

When I called to ask about taking the trip, he interrupted me in mid-sentence, saying, "Be at the boat at 9:30 tonight - bring your own boots and oilers." Then he hung up the phone with a bang. That should have been my first clue.

At the boat, the rest of the gang introduced themselves as we loaded food and ice, and moved gear around on deck. Herb spoke to no one, except to snap orders. He never even said "hello" to me. Well, by daybreak the next day, we had reached the fishing grounds, had our net in the water, and were fishing. Fishing was good. After our first tow, we had two splits and a hoist. That's trawler fisherman talk; it means that the whole crew was up to our crotches in live fish squirming and flipping around on deck.

At this point, I didn't care if the captain was a weirdo. This trip was going to be a money-maker, and that's why I was out here. I was happy - for 2 minutes. The next voice I heard was Herb's. He had the window in the wheelhouse slid down and was speaking to me. He was, at the top of his lungs, addressing my technique of picking through the fish, he also made some direct reference to my work habits and the country of my ancestors which had traditionally produced such laggards as I. As his monologue continued, he also found fault with my hairy face, and my affection for Karl Marx that probably accompanied it. An inverse proportion was noted between the strength of my back and arms and the strength of my mental abilities. He gave a brief history of his experience with men with hairy body types, and finished with some most impolite comments regarding my religious background and that of my family.

While he was ranting on, his head, shoulders, and both arms were hanging out of the wheelhouse. The veins on his neck were distended, and the brim of his hat was bobbing up and down in punctuation of his lecture. Little bits of spittle accompanied his labial consonants and his eyes seemed as big as golf balls. I thought he had suffered a major mental breakdown. My first thought was about how we could get him tied down and sedated somewhere, while one of us got on the radio and called the owner of the boat for further instructions.

The guy picking fish next to me calmly muttered under his breath, "Don't pay any attention to him; he does that to all the new guys on board." I looked at the rest of the crew. They were working along, picking through the fish, acting as if they had not even heard Herb's tirade.

I looked back at Herb. He was staring at me, expecting a response, no doubt. I didn't disappoint him. I opened my comments with a pointed reference to his physical stature and the probable lack of masculinity it represented. (He was about 5 foot, 7 inches tall). His mother's canine pedigree slipped in somewhere; I think it was just before my reference to his IQ and that of all of his ancestors who lived long enough to reproduce. It also seemed appropriate to mention his age (he was about 30 years older than me). In my reference to his age, I footnoted my comments with the almost certain lack of male reproductive functions and capacities which came with such advanced years.

I expressed some concern for the nature of his medical insurance, should he continue to verbally abuse me, making specific reference to the cosmetic dentistry he might need if he didn't leave me alone.

I finally finished with a pointed suggestion that one more word from him to me and I would drag his skinny white ass out of the wheelhouse window and deposit him in the Altantic Ocean around us.

I stopped, out of breath. It was suddenly quiet on deck. The only noise was the grumbling of the big diesel down in the engine room and the screeching of the gulls surrounding the boat as the net is hauled back. My shipmates looked as if they had seen a ghost. Herb's face was twisted up in a wincing snarl. I turned away from him, bent over, and started back picking fish. The other guys did the same. In what seemed like less than a minute, all of Herb's 150 pounds was dropped on my back. Down we went, into the slime and blood of the fish-littered deck. We pummeled each other around the head and shoulders. Not too much damage was done; we both had heavy rubber work gloves on. I do remember we were both covered with fish fluids by the time they got us separated. I also remembered that he bit me on the ear. I still have the scar. I had been bitten on the ear before, but never by a 50-year-old man.

So that was my first meeting with Herb Spinney. As you might guess, we became the best of friends. I soon had rented a room in his house and lived with him and his wife and children for all the rest of the time I fished. They became family to me. We laughed together, cried together, drank a ton of beers together, and, several years ago, we buried Madeline, his beloved wife of 30 years together.

He missed her terribly. He started fishing out of Boston after she died. I think he wanted to spend as little time as possible on the island of Jamestown, Rhode Island, where they had lived. Anyway, he was never the same. In many ways we were closer; I think he felt, in his loneliness, more of a need for an old friend.

Then, a few years ago, a rogue wave washed Herb overboard while he was fishing off Georges Banks one night. They never found his body. Just as well; I can't imagine Herb Spinney buried under grass and trees. And some nights, like the night before last, when the wind is in the east, and I'm standing on the shore, looking over the cold, lonely graveyard of the sea, I think of Herb, of how we first met, and of how I loved him. And sometimes I laugh…

…and sometimes I don't.

A BRAVE WOMAN WHEELS THROUGH LIFE

My brother Richard worked with Sue Schmitt and when she died in 2012, he went to her funeral in Seattle. He told me her story and I had to write it.

Caledonia was the old Roman name for Scotland, along with Britannia and Hibernia, for England and Ireland. So when Col. Samuel McPhail came to Minnesota in the 1800s, it seemed appropriate, given his Scottish ancestry, that he might call the town he founded there, Caledonia.

There it sits today, ten miles away from the Mississippi, a small town of 3000 tucked into the bottom corner of Minnesota, a corner formed by the neighboring states of Wisconsin to the east, and Iowa to the south. Today, across the street from the Caledonia Elementary School is a small street called McPhail Avenue.

Not a lot of famous people came from Caledonia, unless you count Dave Kunst who - some people in Caledonia claim - was (with his two brothers) reputedly the first person to walk around the world. In 1970, they walked to New York City, and being authentic Minnesotans, brought their pack mule along. They left the mule in New York (details unavailable) and picked up a new mule in Portugal. When the third mule died in Australia, Dave thought of giving up, but he met a beautiful Australian who volunteered to pull his wagon with her car. She is today his wife. In 2004, the town of Caledonia commemorated the trek with a plaque saying: "Caledonia: Birthplace of the Earthwalkers David, Peter and John Kunst."

But this isn't a column about the Kunst brothers as steadfast as they may have been. It's about Sue Schmitt.

Born in Caledonia in the late 1940s, Sue Schmitt was a healthy young woman who loved to swim and ride horses. I've been in southern Minnesota; believe me, there's plenty of lakes and horses. When she was 19, a sophomore in college, she was struck down with a neurological disease, unnamed at the time, that moved up her body from her toes, destroying her spinal cord, finally stopping at the level of her chest, leaving her permanently paralyzed. She was unable, because of her severe handicap, to return to the non-handicapped-accessible former campus back in Nebraska; other colleges also refused her.

Finally, Viterbo University in LaCrosse, Wisconsin (just across the river from Caledonia) accepted her, even though their campus was not handicapped-accessible. Before she started classes, a handful of Minnesota carpenters – Sue's cousins – drove across the river and descended on the Wisconsin campus with their trucks, tools, and lumber. These hardy sons of Minnesota, with the Minnesota sense of family, built ramps and a wheelchair lift right there on the campus, and their wheelchair-bound cousin was on her way. She finished at Viterbo, went on to get her Master's Degree from the University of Missouri, and then her Doctorate from Mississippi State, where they constructed the first ramp ever built there for someone to receive a degree.

She travelled extensively to Puerto Rico, Germany, and cruised the Alaskan Coast. She dearly loved and nurtured her grand-niece and grand-nephew. With her indomitable spirit, her work habits and gigantic spirit, Sue's career took off. She accepted a high-level administrative position at the University of Wisconsin, and then moved on to the University of North Dakota. It was at North Dakota where Sue wrote and administrated a massive federal grant from the National Institutes of Health to provide care and maintenance programs for all of the disabled children on all of the Indian reservations on the 70,000 square miles of North Dakota.

Those disabled children gave her a giant star quilt, maybe 50 square feet in area, with each little section made by one of the children. When she left to take her last job as Dean at Seattle University, the quilt went with her and hung in her office there as one of her most precious possessions. And there it hung for the past 16 years until early last month, when Sue's courageous earthly journey came to an end quietly in her van parked outside her office one night at Seattle University.

On a sunny autumn day a few weeks ago at the Church of the Immaculate Conception on the edge of the giant campus, a large picture of Sue was standing at the edge of the altar for her memorial service. Her remains had been cremated as she wished. Hundreds of people crowded the large church, students, colleagues, former students, fellow faculty members and administrators, members of the community...

The Reverend Stephen V. Sundborg, S.J., president of the university presided. His presidency and Sue's tenure on campus began about the same time. He moved slowly down the aisle behind tenured faculty each holding a white lily which they placed in a large vase at the edge of the altar. When he got to the altar, he stopped and turned to face the congregation. He stood there in silence. The Seattle University Choir was rendering "Amazing Grace," "How Great Thou Art," and "In The Garden."

Sue's closest friend, Vida Drew, was also the secretary at her office. They had worked together for so many years. Some may have noticed that Vida was missing this morning. They may have attributed it to extreme grief. Then the music stopped and Father Sundborg seemed to be looking back up the aisle toward the rear of the church.

Some people began to turn slightly to look up the aisle

A PLANNED TRIP
NEVER TAKEN

I've always loved jazz great Bobby Short's music and, in recent years, planned to get down to New York to see him perform. I wrote this right after he died in 2005.

About 100 miles due south of Chicago, on the Vermillion River, Danville, Illinois is just a few miles west of the Indiana state line, and sits on a big vein of coal that, in the 1800s, put Danville on the map. Probably the town's most conspicuous claim to fame is that Abraham Lincoln practiced law there for almost 20 years between 1840 and 1860, until he ran for president.

But Danville is a place known to me because that's the town where Robert W. Short was born on September 15, 1924, the next to the youngest of ten children. As a little boy of 4, Bobby Short began to plink away at the family piano. By the time he was 11 years old, dressed in white tie and tails, he was singing and playing the piano in Chicago, billed at shows there as "The Miniature King of Swing."

The depression was over, and Chicago was the crucible of American black music. Jazz may have had its roots in the South, but it was forged into a coherent form of music in the clubs of Chicago, many of them "legit;" many of them run by the mob. Billy Eckstine, Clark Terry, Joe Williams, Nancy Wilson, and, yes, indeed, Louis "Satchmo" Armstrong, matured professionally in the dark, smoky nightclubs there. Armstrong was born in New Orleans, but moved to Chicago when he was about 20.

So the young Bobby Short was in the right place at the right time. One time he actually teamed up with the famous

Satchmo for a performance. By the time he was 12, Short was a headliner at one of the most famous black jazz venues: Harlem's famous Apollo Theatre. He went back to Danville to finish high school, and then, in 1942, he returned to his first love: music.

He traveled throughout Europe, and spent several years performing in London and Paris. He eventually returned to the United States and made New York his permanent home. He played clubs around the city, making a name for himself, and then in 1968, finally settled in behind the keyboard at the Café Carlyle on 76th Street on the Upper East Side. It seems like a long time ago. John Lindsay was mayor of New York, American soldiers were dying in Vietnam, and Bobby Short was playing at the Café Carlyle.

Watching Bobby Short perform, it was not hard to believe that he had, at the age of 11, performed his first gig back in Chicago dressed in white tie and tails. He continued to be an impeccable dresser, typically wearing a dark suit, white shirt, bowtie, and his signature red carnation in his left lapel. A dapper gentleman, he was the prototype of the sophisticated denizen of Manhattan profiled in the pages of the New Yorker magazine and on the entertainment pages of the New York Times.

And, although he has been the artist-in-residence at the Café Carlyle since 1968, his style and grace have touched jazz aficionados the world over. He has played at the White House for Presidents Nixon, Carter, Reagan, and Clinton. Short's style was appropriate to his attire. He played with a simple elegance and grace that was his trademark. For over 35 years at the keyboard in New York, he sat at the piano and sang the songs of Duke Ellington, Count Basie, George Gershwin, and especially Cole Porter. He was also friends with Leonard Bernstein.

Beginning in the '70s, rock music took over the music scene. By the '80s and '90s, the cult of lip-synching MTV became the norm in the big cities, including Manhattan, and the popularity of performers seemed to be directly proportional to the size of the bank of speakers they had on stage and the decibel level they could produce.

In the midst of this cultural cacophony, one could still take a taxi uptown to the Carlyle on a Friday or Saturday night and step into a quiet oasis reminiscent of a time when both New York and the world were younger and more innocent. A person could sit at a table just a few feet away from the piano, and listen to the non-amplified sounds coming from the keyboard, from the instrument to the ear, with no machine or electronics in between. I discovered the artistry of Bobby Short back in the '70s, shortly after he began his gig at the Carlyle. The first time I heard him sing the Andy Razaf/Fats Waller song, "Black and Blue," I took a deep breath as if to absorb its plaintive beauty.

So last year, I decided to go to New York City, stay overnight and catch Bobby Short at the Carlyle. I had the time; I had the money. I knew he had made some comments about retiring. So I called the Carlyle, got his schedule, checked out the hotel rates, and even got the plane schedules from Hyannis to LaGuardia. And then, well, you know how it is – things got complicated at work, some snags at home, boats to be sailed, countries to be visited, and the next thing I know, it's March of 2005, and I'm remaking plans for my trip to Manhattan to see Mr. Short.

Until I pick up the New York Times this past Tuesday and read that Bobby Short died on Monday. Just like that: dead. So no trip to the Carlyle for me – just another dream that won't come true for a man who let things go, assuming that all things would still be available to him for all time. I'm old enough to know better than that, but I still keep doing it.

This past Thursday night, I sat alone at home and in the quiet of the house, with only the ticking of the clock, I pull down a Bobby Short CD from the shelf. It's his album "Late Night at the Café Carlyle." I look at the clock. It's after midnight. I punch up the music. The house is dark, with only the lights from the stereo system blinking. Bobby Short begins to sing, and I close my eyes.

Minutes later, I'm in New York – at the Café Carlyle. A beautiful woman is by my side; we're at a small table near the piano. I've slipped the maitre d' a small portrait of Ulysses S. Grant to get the table. She's sipping a gin and tonic; I'm nursing a tall chilled martini, straight up with extra olives. He is at the piano, singing the song, "Every Time You Say Goodbye." Our eyes meet. He smiles at us. I look at her. She slips her small hand into my big mitt. I give it a squeeze. Her head drifts toward my shoulder. All is well.

But then the song ends on the CD. I open my eyes, realize that I'm alone in the darkness, and that I'm never going to see or hear Bobby Short play live.

And once again, I remind myself, that if we don't act on our dreams, that's just what they remain: dreams.

A JEWISH MEMBER OF THE FAMILY

I think Howie Fink was one of the first close friends of my own age who died. A man remembers that time in his life when his friends begin to die. This 2001 column is a reflection of that.

I had a bunch of voice-mail messages waiting for me when I returned from Europe a few weeks ago. I had seen the blinker flashing in the darkened office on the night I returned, but I had been on the go, lugging my backpack over my shoulder for exactly 18 hours, so all I was interested in was a hot shower and a warm bed; I could deal with unpacking and listening to phone messages in the morning.

With a long night's sleep, I was up about 5 a.m. I headed for the beach and hiked around for an hour or so, and when I got home, I made a big mug of green tea and honey, sat down in my office, took out a yellow pad and a pen, and pushed the "PLAY" button on the phone machine.

Most of the messages were pretty routine: friends checking in; students checking on final exam grades, etc. Even a call from Europe wishing me a safe journey and a warm welcome home. But one of them stood out in a very ominous way; actually there were two of them – essentially the same message repeated by the same person within the same 24-hour period.

The calls were from the wife of a man very close to me. Now the rest of you old dogs out there know what I'm saying here: when you get a message from a man's wife, it's never - I mean never - good news. I finished listening to the rest of the messages, all of which could be returned at my leisure, but the message from my friend's wife stood large in my consciousness. I couldn't think of anything else. I wasn't ready to return the call, so I tried to putter around for awhile. I split a little firewood in the yard, even tried to finish a short story I had started before I left on my trip. But nothing was able to distract me, so I finally picked up the phone and punched in the 11 digits of the telephone number at the 20-acre horse farm in Swansea, Massachusetts, right up against the Rhode Island state line.

The phone rang five or six times, and the answering machine came on – the wife's soft voice with it's strong Rhode Island accent asked the caller to leave a message. "Prossy," I said. "It's Dan. I've been away in Europe; I just got back last night and I've just gotten your message this morning. I know this is important business, whatever it is, and I'm very anxious to hear from you guys, so call me back as soon as you can. I'll be here all day." Then I hung up.

The phone rang about an hour later. I snatched the phone off the cradle before the first ring had completely finished. She was returning my call.

"Danny," she said, calling me by my boyhood name, "I've got bad news...very bad news..." I don't remember exactly how she said it. I can't quote her words here today. I guess I wasn't paying much attention. Once she said that she had "very" bad news, I knew what was coming next. And she was right; it was very bad news. The worst news of all.

I can remember the first time I met Howie Fink. It was the late 1950s, and I was sitting on a park bench at the Broad Street Entrance to Roger Williams Park in Providence. The park entrance was a hangout for a bunch of us teenage boys from the South Providence area of town. As a group, we represented a pretty wide spectrum of backgrounds, reflective of the neighborhood. We were Italians, Russians, Germans,

Polish, Blacks, Irish and Swedish. We were Catholics, Protestants and Jews. We were athletes, scholars, and drop-outs. But we were all friends.

One day, this dark-skinned, muscular kid pulled up in his car. As he stepped out, a few of the guys greeted him. "Hey Howie! How're ya doin' Howie?" A few called him my his last name. My buddy on the bench next to me, Barry Bellino, said to me, "You know Fink, right?" I told him I didn't. He called Howie over. I stood up. Bellino introduced us. We shook hands.

I remember that he was taller than me and I was over six feet tall. And I remember that, although I had been lifting weights, pumping iron, for a couple of years, his hands were thick and strong. Much stronger than mine. These are things teenage boys notice about each other.

He had a thick head of black curly hair and a big pointed nose that was only accentuated by the heavy black plastic-rimmed glasses that sat upon that nose. His glasses were perfect replicas of the Groucho glasses that you see on sale in joke shops around Halloween. If you wrapped a robe around Howie Fink, gave him a shepherd's staff and a few goats standing around him, he could disappear into the Judean hills around Jerusalem, and as long as he kept his mouth shut, no one would ever know that he wasn't a tenth-generation inhabitant of Palestine.

But there's the rub: the part about keeping his mouth shut. The one time in the very difficult conversation with his wife on the phone when we both laughed was when, in trying to comfort her, I was telling her how very much he loved her, and how their decades together had brought so much happiness into his life.

"I always thought that he'd wind up being a lonely old bachelor," I said. She started laughing on the phone. "Well, if we hadn't met," she said, "He might have been an old bachelor, but never lonely. My god, he'd talk to anyone for hours, wouldn't he?" I laughed with her on the phone, and we agreed that conversation was never Howie's weakness. He could talk the ear off a granite statue.

Howie and I started talking that day over 40 years ago, and never stopped. Howie became as close to being a member of my family as a non-blood relative can be. My mother and father loved him dearly, as did all my little sisters and brothers, who adopted him as another big brother. At Christmastime, he'd put on a Santa hat and beard, and bring little presents to my tiny brothers and sisters. We traveled together; we drank beers together; we got in fights together; we got arrested together.

At his little brother Eddie's bar mitzvah, his father Nathan had the band play "When Irish Eyes Are Smiling" just for me, and I danced with his sister Linda. When my brother Richard was married in the Rockefeller Chapel at the University of Chicago, he asked me to give the sermon at the wedding ceremony. As I stood at the altar looking out over the congregation, I noticed the back doors to the church open and I watched in disbelief as the tall dark-haired man with those funny glasses quietly slipped into a pew in the back.

Like I said, he was a member of the family.

His father, Nathan Fink, the son of Russian immigrants, started selling junk and scrap metal from a wagon shortly after the First World War and, by the time Howie and I had met, he had a big junkyard down on Huntington Avenue, near the corner of Seabury Street. Huntington Avenue is gone, but now and then you'll hear some old-timers in the West Elmwood/Olneyville part of town refer to the Route 10 connector as "the Huntington Expressway."

When the state took the junkyard property for the highway,

Howie and the old man moved the whole operation over to the old Red Bridge over the Seekonk River. Today, both the junkyard and the bridge are gone.

And so is my friend, Howie.

It occurs to me today that, of all my friends, Howie would probably be the only one whose death I would feel compelled to write to all my brothers and sisters about. Each one of them has written back already, sharing their feelings about this funny, serious, quiet, talkative and loveable man.

It also occurs to me this morning that Howie Fink might have been the first man outside of my family that I can say I truly loved. But he was not the last, and that may be the gift that I most remember Howie for.

So, shalom, my dear friend. Say hello to my mom and dad. I know they'll be happy to see you.

A YOUNG COP PAYS THE ULTIMATE PRICE

People often ask if I have a favorite column. That's an impossible question, of course, but I know that this one from 1994 would certainly be in my top ten. It was published in the Providence Journal shortly after the incident it speaks of. The Providence Police Department sent me a powerful reponse, and I was told that the column hung in police headquarters for years; for all I kow, it might still hang there. I didn't know this young policeman, but he was shot and killed in a house a few hundred yards from the front door of my family home in Providence, Rhode Island, in a house where a close boyhood friend once lived. I have been in this house.

The West End of Providence is an undistinguished and forgotten corner of the city, stuck somewhere between South Providence and Federal Hill. It begins somewhere down by the old Hoyle Square near Central/Classical High School and runs along Cranston Street, past the big Armory at the corner of Dexter Street, and ends at the city line by the railroad tracks that run along Route 10, just this side of the old Narragansett Brewery.

In this unremarkable corner of the city is a consistently unremarkable street: Benedict Street. Beginning at the back of the old Providence Gas Company property on Dexter Street, Benedict Street runs up to Cranston Street, crosses it and comes to a sudden stop at the corner of Sorrento Street by the senior citizen housing there. Sorrento Street also stops at the same corner.

There is a reason why both streets end at this point. At one time, perhaps 100 years ago, the area beyond this intersection contained a large pond called Benedict Pond. If you stand at this bitter end of Benedict Street today, and use your imagination, you can see the contours of the old pond running down over Route 10 and up to Union Avenue. It's not clear whether the pond took its name from the street, or the other way around. I suspect that the pond came first.

With the exception of the now-extinct Pilling Chain Co., just off Cranston Street, the length of Benedict Street has always been the typical wood-frame bungalows and the three-deckers that make up many residential neighborhoods in today's New England cities.

When I was a little kid growing up there in the 50s, we knew the name of just about every family in every house. One street over on Potter's Avenue were the Blessingtons and the LaFazias; another block over were the McCoombs. ("Red" McCoombs, a Providence firefighter, died a few years back.) One block the other way, on Wadsworth Street, two doors off Cranston Street, lived Tommy Beard and his kid brother Eddie.(A house painter, Eddie was a Rhode Island congressman several years ago.) On Benedict Street were the Bakers (13 children) and the Venters. My friend Ray Venter's father was an oilman. He parked his oil truck right in the yard next to the house.

Sometimes, guys from South Providence would come over to Bucklin Park to shoot baskets – guys like John Rollins (today a Providence City Councilman) and his cousin Paul. But most of the guys were from a few blocks either side of the neighborhood.

Benedict Street was never a pretty street. Even back then, there were disabled cars parked in the driveways of man houses, and none of the buildings there would ever be used in a Dutch Boy Paint commercial. But the people there, if not exceptional or distinguished, were hard-working and honest folk. Some of the people I mentioned above were black; some were white. It didn't make any difference then and it doesn't now.

The one architecturally significant feature on Benedict

Street is the big tan stone-and-concrete Church of the Assumption. Actually, it is the back of the church that abuts Benedict Street; the front door is one block over on Potter's Avenue. When I walked from my house to the church, the route was along Benedict Street, and then through the side churchyard and around to the front door.

All six of my brothers and sisters were baptized in that church, and each of my three sisters was married in the same building. For 41 years, it was my parents' church. The present pastor, Father Dan Trainor, was raised just a few blocks over, on Sorrento Street. In the early '50s when I was a 10-year-old altar boy, hurrying along Benedict Street at 5 a.m., on my way to serve the first mass of the day at 5:30, I would practice my Latin out loud as I trudged along the dark and abandoned environs of Benedict Street.

The English name Benedict comes from the Latin word for blessing, benedictus, which comes from two other latin words, bene (well or good) and dictus (speaking or saying). A benediction then, is a blessing or speaking well of someone. In the old Latin mass of my boyhood, there occur many variations of the root word, benedictus. Many times over the years, I reflected on the coincidence of the words I was learning and the name of the street I was on as I hustled along the pre-dawn sidewalks of Benedict Street.

The giant stained-glass window in the church, the largest window in the building, is behind the altar. From outside on the street, this massive medieval symbol of faith looks out onto Benedict Street.

On February 3 the serious faces of the saints and mute open-mouthed expressions on the faces of the angels on the stained-glass surface of this giant window were witnesses to something horrible as the looked down onto Benedict Street. They saw the body of a young policeman, Steve Shaw, being carried out of the house numbered 110. Police reported that, during a search of the house, Shaw, a five-year veteran of the Providence Police Department, was murdered in cold blood by Fields, a small-time criminal with a long record. Shaw never even drew his gun.

In his five short years on the job, the well-liked Shaw had been decorated twice with the Police Chief's Medal, and had earned a reputation as a "good cop." He was first Providence cop killed on the job in 66 years.

If, on the morning of February 8, you had visited St. Bartholomew's Church up on Laurel Hill Avenue, you would have been surrounded by men and women in blue, and if you were fortunate to find a seat at Sgt. Steve Shaw's funeral mass there, you would have heard the priest intone the words of The Gloria, one of the four major parts of the Roman Catholic mass.

The first few words of The Gloria would be familiar to you, regardless of your religious background, for they are the words from the first Christmas Eve, words that have appeared in song and in Christmas greetings for 2000 years: "Glory to God in the highest, and on Earth, peace to men of good will."

Then the priest would have continued with the words, "We praise you; we bless you..." and The Gloria continues. In the old Latin mass the phrase "We bless you,' was said "Benedicimus Te."

Walking alone Benedict Street last week, a stranger to this city would have seen the dirty snow piled up along the sidewalk and the paint peeling off the houses, and it might have looked the same as it has for years. But something obscene happened here, something that makes the cold February streets of this city a little colder, and changes this West End street forever. A good man, a good husband, a good cop, was gunned down in an act so senseless, so unnecessary. Gunned down by one of the violent and useless handful among us who change our lives, our neighborhoods and leave us with less.

My this young cop's family be somehow comforted by the fact that it is the Steve Shaws among us who make us better just by being the humans they are. We are indeed blessed to have them amongst us for however short a time. The Providence Police Department has suffered the loss of one of its finest, for sure, but every cop in uniform out on the street today can look down at the black band across his or her shield, and walk a little taller because one of their own was a good cop.

Benedicimus Te, Sergeant Steve Shaw.

The Fathers

ADVICE TO A NEW FATHER

Every father remembers the day he first became a father. This 2003 column tells the story of my first advice to a new father. We have kept in close touch. The little baby described in this piece will be a teenager next year.

I first met Tom when he was a student at Cape Cod Community College. During his first semester there, he took a religion or a philosophy course with me. He was an outstanding student with an instant grasp of the most subtle and difficult concepts and did very well.

Before he got his degree with high honors from Cape Cod Community College, he had taken every course I taught; by that time, we had gotten to know each other very well. As a college professor, I have developed an intuition about which students will someday become friends after they have finished their formal educational experience with me. After Tom was my student for just a few weeks, I knew that we would be lifelong friends. And that has indeed happened.

He went on to a major university after finishing his degree on Cape Cod. We kept in touch by e-mail and telephone, and occasional visits and cups of tea at my house when he was here visiting friends.

He moved to a nearby state. We kept in touch with occasional phone calls. He studied in Europe. We wrote back and forth all the time he was there, and we even managed to have breakfast in Holland one summer morning when I was passing through. Anyway, the years have gone by; Tom is now a man past his mid-thirties, and we have become very close over the close to two decades we've been in each other's lives.

A year or two ago, Tom settled in Boston, and began working there, while continuing his education. A tall and handsome Viking, he is physically fit and has tremendous charisma and people skills. He's one of those young men with so much intelligence and energy that he still isn't sure what he wants to do with his life. But in the meantime, he has worked very hard at a number of career choices, moving from one to another. His work habits and intelligence are such that he will be successful at whatever he chooses to do.

If that sounds like a gift, or a state of affairs you would wish upon your child or grandchild, think again. It's not all it might seem to be: knowing that you'll be good at anything. Believe me, it's the first cousin to knowing that you'll be good at nothing. Anyway, Tom (names have been changed here this morning) called and left a message for me earlier this year. He said he had a problem. He said it was "a big problem" and desperately needed to talk with me. As I recall, it was in the spring.

As I played the message, I could hear the stress in his voice. Like I've said, I know this guy pretty well. I know his face and his body language. And I know his voice. Before I even called him back, I knew that he was in trouble.

I also know that, in my life experience, when young men come to me and tell me they have a problem, the problem is almost always an affair of the heart. Further down the list are problems with work, family, or school, but make no mistake, love is at the top of the list.

The last time I had seen Tom was here on Cape Cod. He was with his friend Priscilla, a beautiful young woman he had met, I believe, in Europe. They had fallen in love, and were making long-range plans for a life together. She seemed to be as intelligent as he, and they seemed to be very taken with one another. I was happy for them both.

Their plans together included some time apart while they decided whether Tom would move to another country, or

Priscilla would come to the United States. As I dialed Tom's number that night, my imagination ran through the litany of things that might have gone wrong between Tom and Priscilla.

Long-distance love affairs can be very difficult; maybe the stress had snapped a few moorings. I also knew that when young people "put off things," those "things" sometime never happen. Much to the dismay of many parents, I'm sure, my advice to young people over the years is of the "carpe diem" variety. "Do it now!" I tell them. My motto is "Leap, and the net will appear." I've had some pretty scary leaps in my life, and even though I'm a pretty scarred-up old bear, I don't know many people who are happier than I.

But the man on the other end of the phone that night was not a happy man. Tom recognized my voice right away and went into his story: During the time that he and Priscilla were working out their future plans, Tom made a mistake. He became involved with Eileen, a woman he met while living in Boston. He had told Eileen about Priscilla, and he thought everything was clear. Well, things were, as they often do, about to become not so clear. To simplify things, Eileen fell crazy in love with Tom and decided that, if she couldn't have him, at least she could have his baby. She deceived him about her birth-control status, and she was now pregnant.

He was angry and confused. Their relationship was, as he put it in a massive understatement, "under a lot of strain." For several weeks, we talked many times into the late night hours. Eileen and he cried together; they fought together. They went to a clinic for abortion counseling. They sought religious advice. They talked to family members. They lost sleep as they tried to decide what to do.

My advice to them was consistent. I told them two things over and over again. One, make a decision now, and stick with it. And, two, remember that you are dealing with a decision that will have a permanent and lasting effect upon three lives.

Then, last week, the phone rang very late at night. It was Tom. I believe he was at the hospital. He was the father of a little girl. He was tired and emotional. "She's beautiful," he said; "Thanks so much for all your help," he said. "You know I love you."

"Yeah. I love you too," I said.

He then asked me if I had any advice. I thought for a few seconds. "Things have changed forever," I said. "This is a day you will remember until you die."

"Yeah," he said thoughtfully.

"And Tom..."

"Yeah," he said.

"Nothing will ever be the same. Ever, ever again."

"I know what you mean," he said.

"No you don't," I said quietly. "No you don't."

And then I said goodnight.

CONSIDERING A SON'S HANDS

When my son asked me to be the best man in his wedding in 1999, I knew I would have to write about it, but I did not know how I would express myself until he gave me a hand with the story.

Until last week, when I thought of his hands, the image that came most immediately to mind was the hands of a little boy: chubby little fingers smudged with the erratic painting of a Cub Scout project on a newspaper-shrouded kitchen table, with the giant and thick muscular fingers of his father intervening and guiding from time to time. In my visual memory, both our fingers are sticky with the half-dried blue, yellow and red pigments of the brushes strewn around the table.

Our hands are again together in the clean-up process. First to the outside deck for a wipe-down with the paint thinner and the old rags from the barn. I take each of those chubby little fingers and caress them with the chemically-soaked and abandoned ragged T-shirt, taking just a few milliseconds more time than necessary to stroke each little digit and clean each little fingernail as an adoring child looks up into my face.

On those occasions, looking down at the fingers of my firstborn, indeed my only, child and performing a ritual that fathers might have been doing from the days when we lived in caves, I often had a sense of the one flesh that exists between father and son. My fingers, his fingers, all mixed up in the process, cleaning my own hands as I clean his, hard to tell who is servicing whom.

There are dozens of other images of those hands of course, and they are present in my reality as well, but the manual ministrations of those single-digit years are the ones that seemed to me to be the most powerful.

Of course I remember the first time I saw and held those hands shortly after his birth. They were like little red and wrinkled carrots, useless and not even attached to the functions of his central nervous system. I watched as those hands developed the miraculous ability to pick up small toys, then went on to the ability to manipulate those toys, and then to his glee and the dismay of nearby adults, the ability to throw the same toys in some general direction across the kitchen or dining room. The immediate screaming response of a dinner guest to a little statue of Rocky the Flying Squirrel landing in his mashed potatoes was sufficient reinforcement, of course, to such behavior, and it was difficult for a father to chastise his son's rapid development of small motor skills.

I remember the hands of a teenager again working with those of his father, helping each other with backpacks in hotel rooms in Italy, on yachts in the Virgin Islands, in the medinas of Morocco, ferries to Nantucket and Vinalhaven, the deserts of Israel, the mountains of the Canary Islands, the big cities of China, and airports, tiny and giant, all around the planet earth.

In the cold mountain passes of more than one January in Scotland, I can see one set of hands squeezing a backpack as the other set of hands pulled on the straps to cinch it even tighter, as if by reducing the cubic area of the pack, one might reduce its weight, knowing that the 50-lb. burden was going to be shouldered for the next six hours.

I also remember, at the end of such days' hiking in the mountains of the Western Highlands of Scotland, being too tired to even shrug the pack from our shoulders, and depending on the other guy to reach his hands under the padded straps and gently slip the perceived 200-lb. pack from the body of his comrade, letting it drop with a massive thump to the floor of some little B&B in a remote mountain village.

Our hands worked together on my boat here on Cape Cod, as well, sanding, painting, and repairing, over the dozens of Mays and Junes of my young manhood and his older boyhood. His hands later pulling protesting blue crabs from the muddy estuaries of Pleasant Bay or landing snapping bluefish from the ocean waters off Nauset Inlet.

Our hands have pushed room-temperature pints of Guinness up against each other with a glassy clang after a long day together, and have slapped each other high fives after Bruin Ray Bourque slipped a puck behind an opposing goaltender with less than a minute left in a tied hockey game, or Nomar Garciaparra went deep into the hole at third and threw a perfect Fenway strike to Mo Vaughn at first, ending a late-inning rally by the Yankees.

However, I wasn't thinking of any of these things as I stood by the waters of Casco Bay in Maine a week ago today. My thoughts were much more on the present.

I was standing in a group of people on the most magnificent day of the year so far. We were standing in a line to have our pictures taken. The breeze was onshore, bringing cool air to green grass at our feet. In the middle of the group, was the bride, her wedding veil softly billowing from behind in the gentle air rising from the blue water spotted with noontime sailors and fishermen.

To her immediate right was her beloved sister, maid of honor, and then bridesmaids, two fellow physicians, close women friends. One the other side of the line were friends of the groom: two childhood buddies from Cape Cod, a friend from Maine, and two guys from Scotland, looking quite comfortable in their kilts and black waistcoats.

And standing next to the groom, to his immediate right,

was the man he had chosen among all the men in his life to be his best man. The professional photographer was waving us closer together, so our bodies were close up against the bodies of the people on either side of us.

As we squeezed together, the back of our hands touched, my right hand, his left. They stayed that way for just a second, their warmth exchanging in the cool air.

And then the large strong hand opened and took mine in a powerful grip, our hands clasped in a union behind the drape of clothing and kilts, in a union invisible to all others on earth. Neither of us moved our heads, but continued to give the photographer our attention as the clicks and flashes went on for a minute or so.

When the wedding pictures are developed, they will show a group of happy people, dressed and elegant. They will show smiles and tangible joy appropriate to a wedding day.

But they won't show everything. They won't show the hands of two men joined in a fierce and powerful grip, each holding on to 30 years of something. Just as well. A picture may be worth a thousand words, but there are some things it cannot capture.

It cannot, for example, capture what happens when the hands of father and son are secretly joined on such a sacred day on the shores of the ever-changing great and blue ocean.

SHARING MY FATHER'S NAME

Having the same name as my father produced some interesting scenarios over the years. This 1988 column mentions a few.

I received a piece of junk mail on Friday which brought back some clear memories. The mail was addressed to: Daniel J. McCullough, Sr.

Now, I know that it's not clear from reading the name next to my picture in the newspaper, but I'm a junior; my father was the senior Daniel McCullough. I was his firstborn, and they were so proud the day I was born that he and my mother decided to name me after him. The first child, a boy - and named after him - how wonderful.

Well, not exactly. There were some days, over the years, when my father wished that my name were Harold or Claude. For example, when I was in college, I became entangled with this crazy artist named Zelda. I don't know if that was her real name or just a nickname, but that was what she called herself, and that was what all her friends at the Rhode Island School of Design called her.

She was an older woman (I think she was around 30). She had this amusing (she thought) habit of calling me on the phone and whispering and crooning to me the most detailed (I mean detailed) descriptions of the most exotic and erotic intentions she had in mind for my immediate future. I mean, she was crazy. She said things to me on the telephone which I haven't, to this day, ever seen in print or on film. I'm blushing right now just thinking of some of those messages.

Anyway, I'm at home with my family one night having dinner. The telephone is in the kitchen where we are all eating. With nine of us using one phone, there was never a time when it rang more than once. With three teenage sisters sitting at the table, often the phone didn't even finish its first ring before a conversation was in place. For some reason, my father was up from the table and was just returning to his seat. As he walked by the phone, it rang.

My father never answered the phone, but he was right there, so....

It was Zelda. She said, "Dan?" My father said, "Yeah." (Our voices sounded a lot alike in those days.) She started one of her monologues. My father just stood there with the phone to his ear; he was gazing off to the other side of the room. His eyes looked like he was trying to focus on a building somewhere in Kansas. It was obvious to all of us that he was involved in a one-way conversation. It looked like maybe someone was telling him bad news; he was so quiet just standing there vacantly staring at a spot on the floor about six feet in front of him.

After a few seconds, he slowly retracted the phone from his ear and, using the receiver as a pointer, gestured to me. "I think this call is for you." he said slowly.

When I got to the phone, she was still talking, continuing to repeat in hot detail what was in store for me the next time she got her hands on me. I interrupted her.

"Hello?" I said.

"Hello, Dan?"

"Yeah."

"Who the hell was that on the phone just now?" she asked.

"My father."

"Your father?"

"Yeah, my father."

"Oh," she said, "I thought it was you."

"Yeah, I know."

I looked across the room at my father. He was staring absent-mindedly into his chowder, stirring it slowly. He seemed to have a lot on his mind.

Another time, the police came to the front door to make an arrest. They had my father all the way out to the cruiser before he was able to explain to them that he was not the guy they wanted.

These guys were city cops; they had heard the "You've got the wrong man - you're making a big mistake" story before, so it took some convincing, but he pulled it off. They had me in custody an hour later.

Things were cool around the house for about a week after that. That's how long it took my father to explain to all the neighbors and their children why two uniformed officers were trying to stuff him into the back of a police car in front of our house.

My favorite story, however, is what my family calls "The Ziggy Hartley Story."

I'm in my early twenties. I'm in college in Providence, but I'm also in the Teamsters' Union, working out of a big terminal not too far from my home. My father is working as a bus driver for the municipal transit authority in the same city. It's a Friday afternoon. I stop by the truck terminal to see if there is any work for the weekend. The dispatcher says, "Yeah, you can take a trip for Ziggy Hartley. He just called in sick. You have to be in Albany by noon, so be here at 4 AM." I'm psyched. It's overtime pay on the weekend.

That night, I go out with my buddies shooting pool and drinking beer. I get in at about 2 AM, set my alarm for 3:30, and go to sleep. When the alarm goes off, I shut it off, put my head back on the pillow, you know, just to get a couple more seconds of rest.

At 4:15 the phone downstairs rings (so they told me later). My mother gets up, wraps her housecoat around her, and goes down to answer the phone in the kitchen.

The voice on the other end says, "This is the dispatcher down at the garage; can I talk to Dan?" My mother tells him to wait just a minute, trudges back up the stairs and shakes my father awake. "Dan, it's the dispatcher down at the garage."

My father, sensing a day's pay at time and a half, rises to the occasion. When he gets down to the phone, the dispatcher (at MY terminal) says to my father, "Hey, are you going to take that trip for Hartley today, or what?"

Now, my father worked for years with a guy named Harry Hartley, he was still driving with him at the time. He was no relation to the Ziggy Hartley I worked with. Thinking that this was indeed, a day's work for him, he quickly jumped into his uniform, got his changebox and stuff, kissed my mother goodbye and headed off to the terminal, leaving me sleeping soundly upstairs.

At 4:30, the phone rings again. Again the voice on the phone says, "This is the dispatcher down at the garage, can I talk to Dan?" My mother says, "Isn't he there yet?" The guy says, "No, and he's got to be in Albany by noon."

My mother thinks, "ALBANY??"

And then all comes clear to her.

She rushes upstairs and awakens me.

Her rush to get me moving in less concern for my timely arrival in New York's state capital than it is concern that I get out of the house before my father returns, making her a witness to a homicide.

Meanwhile, my father, all dressed up in his green company uniform and hat with the badge on it, is involved in a most interesting and personally embarrassing conversation with his dispatcher at the bus terminal.

My mother said later that, although they had been married for over 20 years, she had never seen him in the emotional state as he was that morning when he arrived home at 5 AM, all dressed up and no place to go.

Before my son was born, I told my father that if it was a boy, I was thinking of naming him Daniel, after him. He rolled his eyes and said, "Good luck."

FATHER/SON RITUAL IN MAINE WOODS

Father/son relationships are often tinged with ritual. This 1988 column addresses a ritual my son and I followed for many years until, of course, it stopped.

One of the greatest films ever produced is the film, "Black Orpheus." In 1959; it won the Grand Prize at the Cannes Film Festival, and the Academy Award for the best foreign film of the year. Directed by Marcel Camus, and set in the city and the hills surrounding Rio de Janiero, it is based on the ancient Greek tale of the musician, Orpheus, and his woman, Eurydice.

In the closing scenes of this magnificent film, the main character, Orpheus,is sitting on the edge of one of the cliffs which overlook Rio and face out to the sea, to the east.

Orpheus is an adult hero to the local kids; they believe that he can play his guitar and make the sun rise. For them, it is the playing of the guitar of Orpheus which prepares Brazil for the sunrise. Once Orpheus has finished his morning ritual, the sun may then rise. For them, it is his music which marks the beginning of the day, not the rising of the sun.

Well, my son and I have a kind of ritual for the beginning of summer. It has to do with an annual trip we take to central Maine at the end of May. Until we complete this trip, summer may not begin. We made the trip this week.

After driving 330 miles to a part of New England that most people on Cape Cod have never heard of, we unload our gear at the end of a dirt road in Caratunk, Maine, near the shores of one of the most beautiful bodies of water in New England, Pleasant Pond. We are both tired from the long seven-hour journey as we prepare for our three-day ritual without which summer cannot begin.

We pull our gear out of the back of the truck, unpack our backpacks and set up the tent. The weather is threatening, so we move quickly, with little conversation. This is a routine we have been through dozens of times, and we work together in silence. In minutes, the tent is up; we now have shelter in the Maine woods, and firewood, food and fellowship are in order.

We're into our sleeping bags early; tomorrow is a long day. Our fatigue is a blessing: it makes the hard Maine ground feel soft as a bed in back on Cape Cod.

A half moon is almost directly overhead. It bathes the campsite with a soft white snowlight. The dying campfire sputters and crackles against the chill of the May night. The loons on the pond are earning their name. We reach out and touch each other in a goodnight hand grasp. Our ritual is on schedule.

No alarm clocks necessary here. We are awakened at first light as the deep woods come alive with birds. We crawl out (that's the only verb to describe the human body exiting a tent), throw together a breakfast of whole wheat bread, pepperoni, garlic cheese, orange juice, diet Pepsi, eggs, and kosher half-sour pickles. We get into our wet suits, jump into the truck, punch up some Mozart horn concerti on the tape deck, and we're on our way to the river.

We have been white-water rafting the rivers of Northern Maine since the college senior next to me in the truck was thirteen years old. It's still a thrill, and it has become a ritual. As I've said, summer cannot begin until we hit the white water.

The next four or five hours are spent on the Dead River, white-water rafting with friends of ours from The Forks, a town which sits at the confluence of the Kennebec and Dead

Rivers. Where we put in on the icy-cold River is at about the same latitude as Montreal; the water temperature is in the forties - hence the need for the wetsuits, but it is a beautiful day, and we are glad to be here.

The Dead River is only rafted two days a year. It is what is called a dam-controlled river, which means that the level of the river is influenced by the amount of water which electric power companies or lumber companies choose to release from the dams which they control. Many people put their names on waiting lists a year ahead of time to ensure that they get a trip down the Dead River on one of these two days.

The release today is a pretty good one; the river is fast and in some places, downright dangerous. We spend much time bailing out the raft with an old white plastic bucket wrapped with tape. Around each bend in the river is a new set of rapids, falls, or great standing waves roaring up in permanent protest against the impudence of rocks as big as Volkswagen buses standing in their way. At the end of this day, our backs, shoulders, arms and legs will be tired from paddling and bailing; our throats will also be sore from the screaming necessary to be heard above the roar of the river.

By late afternoon we are back at the rafting base camp, having cold beers and telling stories of this year's trip and the trips of years previous. It has been a full day - familiar, yet different, but full. Our ritual is over; summer may begin.

Later, we are alone back at our campsite up in the woods of Caratunk. The fire is roaring and we are cooking over it with improvised cooking utensils. The circle of light in the center of which we stand drives its radii out into the secret woods around us, and as we stand with our warm faces to the fire, I wonder what creatures might be looking at our cold backs.

We finish eating and gratefully crawl back into the luxury

of warm sleeping bags on ground which is even more comfortable than last night.

We always lay out our tent out on a north/south axis. Before I drift off to sleep, I look out the tent flap and see the Polaris, the north star, directly over the same tall birch tree it stood above last year. I notice that the young tree is a little closer to the stars than it was last year.

And so are we.

MY FATHER &
THE BONELESS CHICKENS

*Every member of my family has a good sense of humor and loves to laugh.
In this 2003 column, I give an example of the source of that sense of humor in
my family.*

A student asked me this week where I got my sense of
humor. Good question. It may be a genetic thing; you
know with the Celtic blood, and all. But my money is on
environmental influences; my father was a prankster all his
life, and when I was a little boy, I worshipped him.

In the afternoon as he came home from work, he'd kiss
my mother at the door, hug me to his side, and head for
the kitchen. He'd plunk his old black metal lunch box on
the table, and open it up to retrieve the thermos bottle and
perhaps an uneaten piece of fruit. And then as he walked to
the sink to rinse out the bottle, he'd began to tell a story from
his work day, as he did most every day.

Not only did the old man have a great sense of humor
himself, but he loved to laugh and make others do the same.
In addition to this, he was also a tireless natural-born story
teller. The main purpose of these after-work stories was to
make my mother laugh. He loved her dearly, and he could
make her laugh as no other human could do. By the time he'd
finish a story, she'd have taken her glasses off, and would have
pulled the corner of her apron up to her face, wiping the tears
from her eyes. As the oldest child, I felt privileged to be a part
of this ritual.

When I was a little kid, I always tried to be there when
the old man came home from work. Partially to greet him and
get a hug, but I think mostly for the stories. I remember one

day he came home from work and told the boneless chicken story.

My father was driving a bus in the city at the time. He had a passenger who rode with him every day, a guy who ran a produce stand at one end of the bus line. He'd drive my father crazy by standing next to the driver's seat and talking incessantly to the old man, until, as he had to do every day, my father would tell him he'd have to take a seat, whereupon the guy would take the seat behind the driver and just continue his monologue.

But it wasn't so much the quantity of the man's discourse that bothered my old man so much as the quality of his daily speech. The guy was a racist, and he'd go on and on about the stupidity, dishonesty, and general lack of character of the people of color who worked for him, as well as the same faults and weaknesses of all minority groups in society.

Now the old man was not an educated man, and he was hardly a liberal. In the '50s, he thought Senator Joseph McCarthy was a hero for going after all those damned communists writers, politicians and entertainers. But he had this thing about race. He was totally intolerant of any kind of racial slur or any speech that demeaned minority groups. When we were children, we'd be better off to use a foul curse word in front of the old man than to use a racial epithet. A curse in front of our mother or little brothers and sisters would get a grab by the collar. But if any hint of a racial term slipped out in front of the old man, the healthiest thing to do would be start running, with the old man up and after you. Most of the people living on my street were black. Even words that we regularly used in our interracial stick ball or street-hockey games were not OK in front of my father. He hated racism in any form, and deeply disliked but tolerated the ignorant racist guy who rode with him.

So one day, the bus comes to the end of the line, and my old man pulls out his lunch box and opens it up. The produce guy is the last one to come to the front of the bus to depart. He asks my father what he's having for lunch. Opening his lunch box, he pulls out two slices of bread, a small container of mayonnaise, and a little glass jar from the supermarket. The label on the glass jar says, "BONELESS CHICKEN."

The old man tells him that my mother has packed him the makin's for a chicken sandwich, that way the bread doesn't get soggy during its six-hour trip in the lunch box. He explains that it only takes him a minute to put the sandwich together and he loves the boneless chicken.

"Boneless chicken?" the guy says. "What the hell is that?"

My father, with his shark-like instincts, senses blood in the water, and swims swiftly in for the kill.

He picks up the jar as runs his finger over the label for the guy. "See, it says it right here: 'BONELESS CHICKEN.' It's boneless chicken. They grow them with no bones," he says with a straight face.

"Grow them with no bones?"

"Yeah," the old man says. "Down on big farms in Connecticut."

The guy expresses skepticism, but not disbelief, as he cautiously asks my father how the little fowl are able to move around, you know, to walk, with no bones.

My father explains, in great detail, the little harness-like mechanisms that each chicken is fitted with to support itself as it grows to adulthood. "They hang them from the ceiling of the chicken houses. You've never seen anything like it." The old man, now on a roll, explains that some American guy brought the idea back from a trip to Mexico in the 1930s.

"It saves a lot of money," he explains to the guy, as he

spreads the chicken meat onto his bread. "They don't have to butcher the chickens, cutting off all the bones and all. They just pluck the feathers and slice them up."

The guy is amazed at this new revelation regarding the advanced state of modern poultry farming, and expresses this amazement to my father, asking the old man what they'll think of next.

My mother and I are gasping at the kitchen table laughing with tears in our eyes, but when my father explains that he was tempted to tell the guy about the boneless cattle they are working on down in Texas, I totally lose it and have to leave the room before I pass out from loss of breath.

Anyway, the guy leaves the bus that day, shaking his head with amazement about the boneless chicken. And the old man told me later that he never saw the guy again. He may have gone home to his wife and/or family and told them about the boneless chicken farms down in Connecticut, and then just watched their faces as silence descended around the dinner table.

But in my imagination, my favorite scenario is his going into work the next day and arrogantly explaining to his minority workers all about the boneless chicken farms, sarcastically laughing and belittling them about their ignorance about such matters.

Yeah, that would be perfect.

The old man would like that, too.

HOLDING HIS SON IN HIS ARMS

Every father has held this horrific fantasy in their mind for just a few seconds now and then. This 2000 column tells the story of a father who lived that nightmare.

Perhaps my favorite photograph of me and my father together is the one I have in my office of the two of us standing together at the head of Town Cove in Orleans. Behind us is my scallop skiff, bobbing at the tide. The old man and I are looking into the camera, both smiling; smiling because that's what you are expected to do when looking into the lens of a camera, smiling also in anticipation of our imminent departure out onto the waters, and, of course, smiling because we are together.

My arm is wrapped around my father, as if I might hold onto him even longer than the eighty-some odd years that he had already spent on this planet, as if, by holding him close enough, I might transfer some of the strength, health and potency of my 49-year-old body into his.

Of course, one might as well foolishly try to stop the rising of the tide behind us in the photograph, as to try and delay the inevitable journey that all of us, including my father, must take when our time here is done. And, sure enough, in a year or so, he was gone, dying as he lived, peacefully and with great dignity in the presence of his bride, in the fiftieth year of their vows to each other.

But he did not take with him the memories of our time together, and especially of the thousands of occasions when I had my arms around him. There are black-and-white photographs showing me, as a toddler, just about able to walk, but holding on to the muscular thigh of my father's right leg, knowing that, as long as he was there to hold onto, all would be well. Me as a teenager, standing with my father in the backyard of our home, holding to my father's shoulders, shovels in our hands, having just completed the erection of a swing set for my little brothers and sisters. The old man and I at weddings, funerals, family reunions, Christmases and summer cookouts.

Even after I became a father myself, and a little boy was holding on to me for dear life as he learned his way around, there were still times I my life when I found great comfort in wrapping my arms around my father, if even just for a moment, and perhaps, just for a moment, becoming a small child again, when everything was clear, everything was free, nothing could go wrong, and my arm around my father was assurance of that.

I think that's why the three photographs of a father and son that appeared in papers across the world a week ago today hit me so very, very hard. The photographs are from Gaza City, a Palestinian town in the so-called "Gaza Strip," a piece of land along the shore of the Mediterranean, maybe 40 miles southwest of Tel Aviv. The Gaza, along with Jericho and some other territories controlled by Israel, was ceded to the Palestinians by the Israelis as part of the peace accords in the '90s.

Gaza City is a seaside community; I have been there many times, and believe me, you would never confuse Gaza City with Chatham or Cotuit. It is a hardscrabble poor place, with narrow dirt streets where the local Arab population gets by with a minimum of services and conveniences. When the Israelis gave Gaza to the Arabs, believe me, they weren't handing over the gem of the Mediterranean. Outside of its strategic value as a buffer between Israel and Egypt, the Gaza is not a place that wealthy people in the Middle East traveled to when they were on holiday.

But Gaza City became even a little less comfortable last week, as fighting between Arabs and Israelis flared up in the streets. And the three photographs I'm talking about were a small flame of that conflagration.

The first photo shows a man, Jamal Aldura, about thirty years old, and his son Rami, 12, huddled behind a concrete block. They are squeezed together, heads down, in a crouch, as if to protect themselves from the cold, the wind, or, as might be appropriate to that part of the world, a sandstorm.

Would that they were protecting themselves from grains of sand. Like sand, what they were huddled against were things, like sand, measured in grains, but much more deadly: they were huddled against bullets. The man and his son were in the wrong place at the wrong time, caught in a crossfire, a virtual storm of shots being fired by Israeli-Palestinian adversaries at each other.

In the second photograph, the man and boy have their heads up and are looking toward the source of the shooting. The man is waving his arm and crying out in Arabic, "The child, the child." Huddled against him, sheltered partly from the shooting, the boy is crying. But, even though he is afraid, his arms are wrapped around his father, holding on tightly. I remember that feeling – holding on to my father and knowing that, as long as I hold on, this will pass; all will be well. But all is not to be well; this story doesn't have a happy ending.

The third and final photograph shows the boy slumped down against his father's leg. The child has taken a fatal shot, killing him instantly. The father is also wounded.

I hold the newspaper in my hands with the three photographs there on the page. I glance quickly from the face of the dead boy in the third photo back up the picture, seconds before, of the alive boy with his arm around his father. Then back down again to the third picture. My eyes flick back and forth. Alive. Dead. Alive. Dead.

It's bad enough that the Israelis and Palestinians are shooting at each other, but that's nothing new: that's what guns were made for – to shoot other human beings. And war is nothing new to anyone old enough to be reading this newspaper. But once in a while, the horror of war comes up and slaps us in the face. For some of us, it's the devastation of the land and resources, for others, the human waste of the bodies of soldiers piled high in post-bellum stacks.

But for me, sitting in my office looking at a framed photograph taken many years ago, the horror of war appears on the page of the newspaper in my hands, in the face of a dead boy, killed instantly, dead in one heartbeat.

With his arms around his father.

TALKING TO MY FATHER

I miss my father. I think about him every day. In this 1990 column, I reflect upon my thoughts two years after his death.

How're you doin' Pop?

I know it's been a long time since we talked, but I've been busy. You know: work, travelling, friends, etc. I know you understand. You always did.

My sister Martha called a few weeks ago to remind me that Mom was having a memorial service for you this Sunday. I told her I'd be there, of course. It's hard to believe that it's been two years this week since you've been gone. After I hung up from talking to her, I called the kid and gave him the date and time. I figure he and I can go together. You know, your two namesakes sitting there while people in the church hear your name (our name) read out loud. I guess there's something fitting about it. I don't know; I don't think much about that stuff.

I notice that the kid still puts a "III" after his name. I don't use the "Jr." much anymore, now that you're gone. I don't know why. Remember when I was little, I asked you to call me "Junior" as a nickname? We both thought that it was a great idea. It lasted about one day until Mom put her foot down and said that no child of hers was going to be called "Junior." Looking back, I'm glad she did that; I know some 50 year-old guys who are still called "Junior," and it's pretty silly.

I spoke to Mom last night. She still misses you a whole bunch, you know, especially around Valentine's Day. I remember those huge Valentine's cards you used to bring her. They were the biggest ones I've ever seen. I remember how you'd come home after work, and give the card to her in the kitchen. She would stop what she was doing, wipe her hands on her apron, sit down at the table, and, with great ceremony, open the card. It seemed to me that it always had a soft fabric heart in the middle. I remember that my little brothers and sisters used to love to rub the soft heart against their cheeks as the card got passed around the room. You sure were quite the lady's man. At least to one lady you were.

She's doing pretty well. I don't think she likes living alone, but that's only a temporary situation. Eileen and Mike have contracted with a guy to put an addition on their house so that Mom can move in with them and have her own space. It should be done in a few months, so she's looking forward to that. I also think that the apartment where you left from has a lot of memories for her and it's probably time for her to have a new environment.

I also told her that the stimulation of having a lot of people around would be good for her. "It'll stop you from getting old," I said. She laughed. I love to hear her laugh. I know that you did, too. You made her laugh a lot, I remember. I think she laughs a little less now that you're gone. Maybe not; I don't know.

The rest of the family are doing fine. Everyone's healthy and reasonably happy. All of the brothers and sisters manage to keep in touch, almost on a weekly basis. Even if we are not personally in touch with each other, each of us speaks to someone who has spoken to someone else, etc., so there's a chain of communication among us.

I forgot my sister Mary's birthday in January, a few weeks ago. I sent her a belated card, a funny one. What other kind of card could you send Mary other than a funny one? Eileen's birthday was last week; Martha's is next week. Bobby and Tommy's were in January. Richard and I are the only summer babies, with our June birthdays, me the firstborn of all your babies.

Remember how you used to say out loud, in public, that you and Mom were married on June 11, and I was born on June 30? Mom would blush and quickly explain that the two Junes were one year apart. You would just laugh and say, "Well, it's still true!"

Boy, you wouldn't believe how the grandchildren are growing, all sixteen of them. I need to warn you that some of them are bringing boy and girlfriends home to meet the parents. I think that some of these people are getting "serious," if you know what I mean. There could be weddings. You could be a great-grandpa one of these days. I guess that also means that one or more of us could be....is it possible.... grandparents? Good grief!

So, how am I doing?

Yeah, I'm doing fine. I really can't think how life could be much better. I love my work; you know how important teaching is to me. My personal life is about as good as it's ever been. I love my friends. People are good to me. My writing is coming along fine. Actually, I should tell the whole truth: I should be working harder on my writing, but you know how I am. I remember how you used to shake your head and laugh at me and say that no one could ever say that I wasn't enjoying life as I went through it. Well, I haven't changed much; I'm still taking time to smell the roses, as they say.

Well before I close, I do want to tell you that I think of you often, pretty much every day, I guess. I can't say that I miss you, certainly not in the way that Mom misses you, but it would be real good if maybe tonight, or one of these nights, you could come back, maybe just for an hour or so. I wouldn't keep you long, and I wouldn't have a lot of heavy, serious things to say. As you know, we said all those things before you left.

But we could get in my truck and take a ride down to the beach. Just for awhile. Orion would be high in the southern sky, and the February wind would be in the sou'west - just for us, just for an hour. We might not even talk at all, maybe just walk along side by side, and I could look into your blue eyes again and watch your white hair blowing in the starlight. I think that would be enough, then you could go back.

Do you remember when my buddy John Lynch's father died? We were all in high school at the time. I think I was a pall bearer at the funeral. I remember that after one of the wakes, he and I were alone with the casket. "Hey Mac," he said.

I turned to him. "Yeah?"

"They're a long time dead," he said, looking at the casket. "They're a long time dead." I never forgot that moment or those words. I think that's what I would say to people whose parents are still alive today. "Remember, they're a long time dead."

So that's it for now, Pop. I think when I finish this, I might take a ride down to the beach, anyway. The wind is in the sou'west and Orion is high in the southern sky.

And who knows, maybe you'll be there.

...just for an hour or so.

The Laughter

REGGIE GETS A NEW POINT OF VIEW

This 1999 column can still make me laugh, as I remember Reggie the dog acting like one of the guys he hangs with.

Last winter, a friend and I had gone to the coin-operated laundry in Orleans to do my laundry. Like most guys who do their own laundry, all of my white and gray clothes have a nice pink tinge to them, and my friend, noticing that laundry skills were not my long suite, had volunteered to help and instruct me in this area.

We had sorted the clothes into different piles. Did you know that you are supposed to keep colors and whites separate from one another in the washing machine? Well you are. And we were doing it that night. The two washing machines had been filled, soaped and started in their cycles, so we had about 40 minutes to kill.

A draft pint of Guinness worked its way into our conversation. A couple of hundred feet either way, the laundry is halfway between the two best pubs on the Lower Cape: The Land Ho! and the Yardarm. Both offer the Guinness. We walked out the door of the laundry and stood there for a minute, trying to decide.

Forty minutes later, we were walking back across the parking lot of the laundry. The Guinness was perfect. One of us had two pints, the other had one. Perfectly fortified, we were ready to deal with the big industrial-sized rotary dryers inside.

It must have been about ten or eleven o'clock at night in the middle of February. When we left earlier, my truck was the only one in the lot. As we approached the restaurant, we noticed another truck had arrived, and, as we passed, I saw that it belonged to my buddy Eddie. In the heavily smoke-filled cab of the truck he sat there with his brother, Scott and their dog Reggie. Eddie and Scott were smoking a cigarette – the same cigarette – and were passing it back and forth to each other, each pass going directly in front of Reggie's nose. I could hear the bass thumping ba-doom, ba-doom, of a loud rock tune even though the windows of the truck were rolled up tightly.

Inside, in the heavy cloud of smoke, Reggie was sitting up on the front seat between them, staring straight ahead at the bright lights of the laundry that spilled out into the dark winter night of the parking lot. He seemed to be focused on something inside the building, maybe a cat or a kid or something like that. I remember turning to look in through the big front windows myself to see what Reggie was focusing on, but the place was empty.

Scott rolled the window down and shouted a cheery and hearty greeting above the sound of the rock music as we came alongside. A big blast of the heavy sweet-smelling smoke wafted out into the cold clear air. We talked for a few seconds, Eddie and Scott seemed to find every thing I said pretty funny, but Reggie just kept staring straight ahead.

Scott extended his arm out the window with a stubby hand-rolled cigarette in his fingers, offering us a drag. We waved off the generous offer, and headed back into the building. We started to transfer my laundry from the washers to the dryer. Did you know that you don't have to separate colored from white clothes in the dryer? Well, you don't.

While we were busy with our chore, Eddie, Scott and Reggie came in, moved some of their own stuff from washer to dryer. Reggie seemed a little unsteady on his feet, and Eddie and Scott were the happiest laundry washers I'd ever seen. Theh two guys headed back out to the truck to continue smoking. As the door closed behind them the room became silent again, except for the grinding of the machines.

A few minutes later, I had occasion to cross the room, and was startled to see that my friend and I were not alone. Reggie was still there, sitting in front of the big dryer with the guys' clothes inside. At first, he looked like a watchdog, sitting there, staring at the glass window of the dryer, guarding the clothes. There are always stories of things being ripped off at the public laundry, and I was impressed that man's best friend was still, even in these modern times, guarding the possessions of his master.

I looked out through the windows of the building where Eddie and Scott were happily bobbing their heads to the throbbing of the music in the truck, six feet away from the front door. I could hear the music from where I was standing despite the fact that it was inside a closed truck and I was inside a closed building, with two big machines going. I was really concerned about their damaging their ears.

As I caught their eye, I pointed to Reggie, dedicatedly guarding their clothing, and gave them two big thumbs-up signals. They both opened their mouths, showed me all their teeth, nodded their heads enthusiastically, and returned my communication with four thumbs up from inside the truck.

I guess it was then that I noticed Reggie's head moving, ever so gently, ever so rhythmically. You'd have to look pretty close to see it, but it was there. Was he bobbing to the music? No way. Music is just noise to dogs. The noise of the machine? No, that wasn't the motion. My friend came over to join me in the Reggie watching.

Then we saw what was happening. Reggie had locked onto a bright piece of clothing - it looked like an orange-colored shirt - just as a jet fighter pilot can lock his heat-seeking radar onto another aircraft. His nose was pointed at the shirt and was moving in a small circle corresponding to the large circle the shirt was describing inside the machine. Other than that slight movement of his head, he could have been one of those concrete poodles that people in Cranston, RI, have on either side of their front doors. The rest of his body was rigid as a piece of furniture.

This past Thursday, I told this story to a friend who knows a lot about dogs. He explained that, to Reggie, it was the same as if he himself were moving. That's why he was concentrating so fiercely, just as a human might do racing downhill on skis.

A fast downhill ski trip for a quarter. Not bad. A dog's life might not be so bad after all. At least not for a few minutes on a cold, but smoke-filled, January night.

GRAND LARCENY: ELEPHANT

This piece was in the Cape Cod Times in 1991. It details one of the many failed attempts to engage in a life of crime as a young man. I have often wondered how the story might have ended if the visitor in the car had arrived 20 minutes later.

I was working as a commercial fisherman in Narragansett Bay. The fog was very heavy this particular summer morning just after sunrise, and we had tied up the boat at a big dock, to have another pot of coffee waiting for the sun to rise higher in the sky and burn off the morning sea fog, as it always did.

The dock we tied to was at a big shore-side amusement park called Rocky Point, totally empty at this time of day. We had a crew of eight including our captain. My buddy Frank Glawson and I were in our early twenties; the rest of the gang were at least 20 years older. We were both strong. – Frank was potato farmer muscle; I was weight-lifter and hockey player muscle. One night in a bar in Point Judith, Buddy, our captain, was talking to another captain. He thumbed over at Frank and me sitting next to him and said, "These two guys could pull the side off a barn." So we were valuable crew, but our fellows thought we were crazy. Well, maybe they had a point. You can decide as you read on.

It was a hazy and foggy early summer morning on Narragansett Bay. Frank and I were fishing on a boat called the Menco, a sturdy old Western-rigged trawler. As a matter of fact, I believe the Menco is still fishing out of Provincetown. We were seine fishing for pogies, or menahaden. As a matter of fact, the Menco had gotten its name from the name of the fish, the menhaden.

We were doing pretty well, averaging over 100,000 pounds

a day. We had landed almost a million pounds the week before. We had an airplane pilot, who flew low over the water, found the schools of fish, and directed us to the fish by radio.

But this particular morning, as I've said, was foggy and hazy. The sun had been up for about an hour; we could feel it through the haze. It was about five a.m. The pilot couldn't fly because of the limited visibility and low ceiling. There was no sense in our looking for fish ourselves; I had climbed to the crow's nest high at the top of the mast, and could just about see the deck below, much less schools of fish in the water. The captain decided to go and tie up alongside the big dock at Rocky Point Amusement Park, and wait for the weather to improve. This was a common phenomenon; by 8 a.m. the sky would be clear, our plane would be in the air, and we'd be able to go back fishing.

We secured the lines at the dock and killed the big diesel engine. In the still of the heavy mist, the only noise heard in the early morning air was the cries of distant gulls and the crackling of the radio as we waited to hear from the pilot sitting on the runway at Greene Airport, eight miles and as many minutes away. Some of the gang started a pinochle game. Some drank coffee. Our captain, Buddy Fredette, crawled back into his bunk and dozed. I mention here that Frank and I had taken as our mission for the summer to drive him crazy with practical jokes, etc. Once, we put a <u>very</u> realistic rubber snake in his bunk; we also filled his sugar bowl in the galley with salt. You get the idea. The plan was working pretty well; he had a giant bottle of Tums right up next to the compass at all times.

Frank and I decided to take a walk up through the deserted early morning grounds of the sprawling amusement park. It was kind of creepy, walking along through the deserted midway of brightly-colored display stands, among the silent carousels and Ferris wheel frozen in place. Other than the morning birds, we were the only living things in the park. Or so we thought.

Frank and I hadn't gone far when we turned a corner and came face to face with an elephant. He stood about seven feet tall at the shoulder. He was chained to a big post in the ground. The chain wasn't very heavy duty for an elephant. Back to the chain in a minute.

Frank nudged me ahead of him as we got closer to the elephant. When we got closer, I tentatively reached out my hand toward him. He responded by rubbing his trunk up and down my arm. Minutes later, we were standing right beside him, rubbing and talking to him.

Then she made a move toward several bales of hay, but couldn't reach them because of the leg chain attached to a stake in the ground. I tore off the plastic covering on one of the bales and started feeding her. Frank turned on a spigot attached to a hose and started watering her. You wouldn't have to know elephant language to know the sounds that a happy elephant makes. It was like a small foghorn miles away.

I looked down at the chain on her rear foot, and I got an idea. I should mention here that although Frank was just three years younger than I, he was raised on a potato farm in rural Slocum, a small town deep in the hinterlands of central Rhode Island; I was raised in the inner city neighborhood of Providence. My ideas for pranks to drive our captain Buddy crazy were pretty extreme, and Frank loved them. He was putty in my hands.

"Frank," I said, "Go back to the boat and get the bolt cutters."

"Oh, no," said Frank. "What will we do with her?"

"We'll just walk her back to the boat to meet Buddy

and the crew," I said calmly, as if stealing an elephant were something I did twice a week. "It'll make Buddy crazy!"

Frank was back in minutes with the bolt cutters. He was holding the chain tight while I was trying to cut it. The three of us were totally engrossed in our work. No one more interested than the elephant who watched, silently looking back at the chain and the bolt-cutters as we labored. I wondered what he was thinking.

So engrossed were we in our work that, at first, I didn't hear the soft crunching of tires on the gravel behind me. Then the sound of an automobile engine idling. I turned slowly. A fourth set of eyes was also very focused on what we were doing. The first thing I saw was the black and white markings and the lettering on the car that spelled out "P-O-L-I-C-E."

"Morning, boys," the cop said nonchalantly, his elbow nonchalantly resting on the open window. "Whatcha up to?" The question was, of course, totally rhetorical. It was pretty clear what we were up to. The cop nodded toward the back seat and said two words: "Get in."

He delivered us to the boat. We thanked him. He said nothing. We told Buddy the story later in the morning. He didn't believe us.

Just as well. The Tums bottle was almost empty.

WAITING FOR A MARKED MOUSE

In this 2011 column, I felt a little better after hearing about another guy's encounter with the skunk and the squirrel.

The comments ranged from my buddy Brian's simple statement, "You're crazy," to my friend Annie's sympathetic, "It doesn't seem possible, does it?" But even in gentle Annie's comment, I knew she was thinking: "I love this guy, but he's nuts."

By Wednesday, I was beginning to weaken. Maybe I needed to think twice about this, since absolutely nobody believed me.

But on Wednesdays, I work with my two partners Maureen and Karen. We've met each other's families and life partners, and over the years we've worked so closely together, we've become like brother and sisters.

I love these two women dearly and trust them completely.

By mid-morning, I couldn't hold it in any longer. We had spent some time hacking through the brush off Willow Street in Hyannis, across from the railroad tracks. We use hand-held pruning tools to cut thorny vines as we move through the woods. Soon we were back to the road. Standing in the parking lot, before moving on to our next venue, we put our tools away, checked each other for ticks and examined little tear-marks from thorns on our shirts.

I began to tell my story as we climbed back into the black Jeep. When I finished, Maureen said nothing. Karen looked like she was deep in thought. And I figured, here it comes, more ridicule and abuse.

And then Karen began to speak. When she was finished, I realized I had finally found someone who might find a grain of truth in my story. If she weren't driving along Route 28 at 40 m.p.h., I would have reached over and hugged her.

She told me the story of her father's encounter with the skunk and the squirrel. You see, her father had this skunk and a squirrel who kept...

Wait a minute... I just realized I'm getting ahead of myself here. You'll need a little background to get the significance of the skunk and squirrel story. I'll get back to the skunk and squirrel in a minute.

Three or four months ago, back in April, I told a story on this page about a little mouse who had spent a good part of the winter in my house. I had nicknamed him Algernon. By April, he was becoming a nuisance. I trapped him in one of those humane little traps that don't kill the animal. Then in the morning, I released him to the woods and marshland behind Nauset Beach in Orleans, 4.1 miles from my house. End of Algernon.

Maybe.

A few months pass, and early last Tuesday morning - the day before I work with Karen and Maureen - I'm alone quietly reading on the bench in my living room. Out of the corner of my eye, I see movement. I look to my right. It's Algernon. He's back. I can tell he recognizes me; he has stopped in the same spot behind the Morris Chair and made eye contact with me just as he used to all winter long.

I set the trap, and in a few hours, he's in the little cage; I get a good look at him. His face is the same. I know it's him. I haven't time to deal with him today. I put some crackers, cheese and water in the cage, and put him in a cool dark corner of the house until tomorrow. Then I make the mistake of telling people it's the same mouse.

That's when my troubles began. The two major sources of ridicule heaped on me were: 1) The 4.1 miles which one wag estimated to be about 200 mouse miles, and 2) My certainty that the current mouse was indeed Algernon.

Okay: Back to Karen's father, the skunk and the squirrel:

A skunk was becoming a nuisance around his yard. Karen's father trapped it in a humane trap, covered the trap with a box and delivered the skunk from Hyannis to Yarmouthport, maybe six miles away. He did the same for a pesky squirrel from the back yard.

Soon a skunk and then a squirrel returned to the yard. Much to his friends' and family's disbelief, Karen's father claimed that it was the same two animals. Nobody took him seriously, much for the same two reasons that people ridiculed me: the distance and the identification of the individual animal.

Undaunted, he trapped the skunk again, but this time took some bright yellow paint and marked the skunk before delivering it one more time from Hyannis to the North Shore of Cape Cod. He did the same for the recaptured squirrel.

Well, the skunk was later found dead by the road, but he was on a line between the place where he had been dropped off and Karen's house, maybe halfway back. The squirrel actually made it back to the house next door.

I feel vindicated after hearing Karen's story.

Getting home that afternoon, I prepare to run a few errands including delivering the mouse to a different marsh and woodland than the first time.

I've got the well-fed and caged Algernon on a kitchen chair, ready for his excursion. I then remember I've a small box of junk in the cellar to be brought to the dump. I go to get it.

The can of spray paint in the box is almost empty. The

color is that fluorescent orange that surveyors use to make marks on the highway or trees. I hold the can in my hand for a few seconds.

I'm thinking thoughts I shouldn't be thinking...

The paint-soaked Q-Tip fits perfectly through the mesh in the cage. Algernon jerks a little as the wet cotton touches his right hip, leaving a tiny bright orange dot there, smaller than a lentil. I turn the cage around and do the same on his other hip.

Ten minutes later and miles away, I give the open cage a shake and he scurries through the dry brown grass, two little orange taillights going with him.

I'm waiting.

Today is day eleven.

A GAME OF MUSICAL CHAIRS

I'm a sucker for practical jokes, so when my friend Leslie told me this story, I had to include it in a 2011 column.

My friend John and his partner Leslie were on Cape Cod last weekend. On Friday, at Cape Cod Community College, I had a one-man show, reading some of my writings, and they had driven up from Connecticut to be there.

I love him a lot. John and I have been friends for 45 years. My son calls him "Uncle John," and his children, even to today, refer to me as "Uncle Dan."

He and Leslie live down in a beautiful little village west of Hartford. He's a writer, mostly having worked for newspapers, including the Baltimore Sun and several large Connecticut papers. Today he's employed by a big insurance company, writing and editing internal and external communications; mostly writing speeches for the President of the company.

They were going home on Sunday morning, so Annie and I planned a quiet dinner with them Saturday night in Orleans. They are a fun-loving couple. John, like most writers, is a wonderful story teller. A career journalist, he has an excellent sense of timing in telling stories and loves to laugh himself. Leslie is also a live one. When I picture her, I picture her laughing. This story is about her sense of humor.

We lingered over an elegant dinner, and as the evening wore on and coffee was being sipped, we got talking, and the topic of practical jokes came up.

Leslie told a side-splitting story about a big annual banquet held by an insurance company she worked for until recently. It was a dress-up fancy affair with awards given out and short speeches by executives of the company, and it went on for hours.

Her boss was a humorless guy with not much of a creative streak. His plan for the dinner was to sprinkle the "fun" people, the "creative" and "lively" people across the room, so that they might lighten up the evening and maybe stimulate conversations among the less interesting people. He did this by assigning seating at the dinner. He placed fancy little name tags at each place, you know, like they do sometimes at weddings.

Now when you think of a large banquet hall filled with mid-level insurance company executives, you probably don't think of a room filled with stimulating, sophisticated, artistic or literate people laughing as they slap their thighs and exchange high-fives. As Leslie told her story, it would appear that such a generalization might be accurate.

She and a handful of her friends were known in the company as lively jokesters, always ready to break the ice when conversations went cold. They also had interesting lives outside the company and were well-rounded personalities.

They dreaded the plan that their boss had for breaking the fun-lovers up and distributing them across the large dining room. It just seemed so artificial.

The previous year, the dinner had been awful, as Leslie and her friends sat at separate tables filled with the most boring and dull people imaginable, each hand-picked to be at each table by the boss who saw his plan as a mark of his human engineering genius. Now and then, as they glanced across the room, the friends would see each other and roll their eyes or place their palms on their foreheads in universal non-verbal communication.

This year, on the afternoon of the evening banquet, hours before the dinner, the boss would go through the dining hall with a roster of names and a box filled with name-tagged table cards corresponding to the names on the dinner roster. Alone in the room, he slowly went table to table, picking out the personalities that he wanted to mix with each other, once again separating Leslie and her friends from each other across the room. By mid-afternoon, the cards – and his plan – were in place.

That evening, people would come in, find their name tags, and settle in for the annual banquet.

Leslie isn't sure exactly how this happened, but this year she and her girlfriend stole their way into the banquet hall, maybe an hour or two before the dinner was to begin.

They had a plan.

Right.

It was risky. If they got caught, it would not go well for them. They might not get fired, but they would definitely be on the wrong side of their boss. Probably for quite a while.

But they courageously went ahead anyway, moving from table to table, picking up cards reading then out loud to each other across the room. In less than an hour, the seating system for the room had been totally rearranged. Their boss' master plan had been completely rewritten and all the crazy fun-lovers were together at two adjacent tables, and not spread across the room according to the boss' plan.

They quickly made their getaway without being caught, and several hours later they reappeared at the big dining room, all dressed up for the annual banquet. They found their ways to their assigned places and acted totally surprised – as did their friends – to find themselves surrounded by the fun folk of the company.

Now and then, they'd sneak a look at the big boss at the head table as he began to notice that something was amiss. I think she told me that, at one point, he actually strolled casually around the room before dinner, unobtrusively glancing sideways over his shoulder as he passed various tables. He must have been thoroughly confused.

Meanwhile, Leslie and her friends had the time of their lives at the best dinner yet, trading stories of trips to the Metropolitan Museum, recent books read, or interesting new yoga classes opening up.

At nearby tables, other employees were discussing rider mower models, recent surgeries, or passing around pictures of their children.

Now and then, someone would look around the table and wonder how it ever happened that the boss would put this group together. Leslie and her girlfriend just shrugged their shoulders, shaking their heads in sympathetic amazement at how such a wondrous thing could have occurred.

THE MYSTERY OF THE BABY SOCKS

My former roommate still doesn't know the secret of the baby socks as told in this 1998 column.

Oh, man, this must be international footwear month.

First off, not long ago, a friend asked what a single odd sock was doing hanging on the hook on the back of my bathroom door. I explained that when a sock disappeared, leaving a single sock in the laundry, I simply hung the orphan sock there until that happened again, and then I just put the two orphan socks together in a lovely marriage, and then carry on with my life and with no single sock hanging on the towel rack. You know, until another orphan shows up in the washing machine.

Now, I don't know where the socks go. Maybe to a fourth dimension of space/time in another universe. Maybe they are stolen by sock gremlins. Maybe they go to Socks Heaven. Maybe they are all in Arkansas at a big home for orphan socks. Like I said: I don't know.

Those of you who have met me personally know that I am no slave to fashion, so an unmatched pair of socks on my feet on any given day is not a sartorial tragedy for me. In my college lectures, my students often note a mismatch of style or color in my socks. They probably think, "Well, he's an absent-minded philosophy professor; what can you expect?"

To this date, however, I have managed to always wear a matching pair of shoes. On the day when I show up with a work boot on one foot and basketball shoe on the other, I hope someone makes a phone call to the proper authorities to see that I'm taken to a place where I will receive some compassionate care.

A buddy of mine who studied at Oxford told me a story about some students sneaking one night into the office of a very old professor there, and painting beautiful flesh-colored bare feet on his rain boots, highly detailed with toes and toenails exquisitely done. After the paint dried, they covered the boots with water-soluble dull boot-black, then replaced the boots in the corner of the office at the foot of his umbrella rack.

The first rainy day after that (you don't have to wait long for a rainy day in Oxford, England) the old professor put on his boots and started across campus in the rain. He hadn't gone very far when the boot-black washed off, giving passersby the impression that he had gone over the edge, and was now walking barefoot across campus in the November rain.

I wish I had thought of that.

But I do have a pretty good sock story.

After explaining the orphan socks on the back of my bathroom door, I told my friend the story of the baby socks.

My buddy Jim and I were roommates years ago in Boston, when I was in law school at Boston University; he was also in law school. We lived in an apartment building up on Myrtle Street on Beacon Hill, and were the prototypical odd couple.

Jim was a neat, clean, spit-shined ex-Marine. I was a not-so-neat, ex-commercial fisherman. I don't have to tell you who was Oscar and who was Felix.

To save a few bucks, and to get a free meal, Jim would regularly drive out to the suburbs of Boston to do his laundry at his sister's house. The mother of several infant children, she had a big industrial-sized washing machine and dryer.

One night, having returned from his laundry trip, he is folding and putting away his laundry, telling me about the lovely gourmet meal he had at his sister's. I'm sitting at our small kitchen table, staring into a ketchup-laced bowl of leftover Campbell's baked beans.

Suddenly he exclaims, "What the hell is this?" He holds a small baby sock in his hand, obviously from the washer or dryer at his sister's house. We laugh. He returns the sock on his next trip.

The next day, I'm walking home from BU. I pass by a children's specialty store on Newbury Street. There's a sale going on. Satan and all his angels take possession of my immortal soul and force me down the few steps into the shop. Those same evil forces twist my will until I am powerless; I produce money from my pocket, and engage in commerce with the woman behind the counter.

I leave the store with three little pairs of baby socks. I remember they were blue, yellow and pink.

Returning from his next trip to his sister's house, he comes out to the living room holding a freshly washed and dried yellow baby sock up in his fingers. We both laugh. He returns the baby sock to his sister, who claims she didn't recognize it.

After his next trip, Jim's laundry had a nice baby-blue sock in it when he returned to Beacon Hill. His sister didn't recognize that one either, and now had two odd socks.

Every time he'd return from the sister's house with a big duffle bag of laundry, I'd sneak a new sock in the bag while he wasn't looking.

One time, at the YMCA on Huntington Avenue, a baby sock in one of the legs of his sweat pants fell out on the floor of the men's locker room as he dressed in front of some other macho guys. A nice pink one, that time.

It was making him crazy. I overheard a conversation between him and his sister one morning about the socks. I had to get up and leave the table, lest I blow my shredded wheat out through my nose, laughing.

It amazed me that it never occurred to him that the socks might be originating in Boston. He was certain that they came from his sister's laundry room.

I soon ran out of socks; I never told him the truth.

But every time I lose a sock in the laundry, I'm a little suspicious.

Nobody knows better than I do that these things don't always happen by accident.

A STORY OF TWO ORATORS

Some incidents from childhood are as clear decades later as if they happened yesterday. This 1987 column tells of one such incident in my life.

While going through some old photographs this week, I came across a photograph of my fourth-grade class from the inner-city parochial school where my education began. Two cherubic faces grinned out at me from the group.

Those two faces belonged to me and to Bobby Cooper.

As I looked at the picture, taken toward the end of the school year, I thought back to a day about a month before when I would not have given Cooper a fat rat's chance in hell (as we used to say in fourth grade) of ever living to see the springtime of his ninth year.

I guess it all started when our home room teacher, Sister Mary Andrew, announced one day that the SUPERVISOR was coming next week. The SUPERVISOR!

Good Lord! The word itself was enough to galvanize the class into frozen terror. The Supervisor was like a head nun from the Bishop's office – sort of an Inspector General. She came around once a year to check on the schools in the diocese to make sure that.....well, I'm not really sure what she wanted to make sure of, but I knew that whatever it was she came to make sure of, if, when she left, she hadn't been made sure of it, heads would roll.

Anyway, she's announcing the Supervisor's visit, and telling the class that two students will be chosen to recite poetry when the Supervisor visits. She then asks for volunteers. You had to be there, but this would be the modern equivalent of asking for volunteers to walk naked with an armful of uncastrated tomcats through a pitch-black garage full of AIDS-infected pit bulls.

So, Cooper and I are gesturing to one another, you know, each pointing to the other guy and chuckling about reciting poetry. Cooper and I are in our own world, but, with one ear, I hear her say that she has two volunteers. As I turnaround to see who the unfortunate idiots are, I hear her say, "Mr. Cooper and Mr. McCullough."

You have perhaps heard the expression about having a smile wiped off your face. Well, I looked back at Cooper; he was white - even his freckles looked lighter. I felt like I had swallowed a live snake.

The next week was a blur of memorizing lines of poetry. "I chose "Trees" by Joyce Kilmer. Cooper wouldn't tell me what he had chosen, but on the morning we were to recite, he told me with disconcerting cockiness that he was sure that Sister and the Supervisor would like both of them.

Both of them!! I almost died. He had memorized TWO poems!! I was a goner. Done in by my best buddy's ambition. I couldn't believe it. I was sick.

The moment of truth came: Cooper was called first. He strode to the front of the room, confident and self-assured. I was terrified, going over and over my own lines about Joyce Kilmer's tree.

I looked up as Cooper started to recite. His words started out across the room:

"A curious bird, the pelican. His beak holds more than his belly can."

There was a pause, a long pause. The Supervisor looked at Sister Mary Andrew; she looked back at the Supervisor. Cooper looked straight ahead, beaming and sure of himself. He even took a little bow before he sallied forth, clearing his throat as if he were a Roman orator and saying "Poem number two."

He continued: "I never saw a purple cow. I never hope to

see one. But one thing I can tell you now: I'd rather see than be one."

I knew at that moment that Cooper's family would have a quiet get-together on his next birthday. His picture would be on the dining room table. They would speak in hushed tones of their late son, Bobby.

He was dead meat, I knew it; the class knew it; Cooper didn't know it. The Supervisor was fidgeting, Sister Mary Andrew was chewing on her bottom lip and squinting at Cooper as if she were staring into the sun.

Then, as he did earlier, he took another little bow and headed for his seat. He never made it. Before he got there, Sister had him by the back of the neck and propelled him down the center aisle of desks and out the back door of the classroom. Roger Thibault, who sat in the back row, later swore that Cooper's feet never touched the floor on the way down the aisle.

She came storming back into the classroom, dropped into her seat next to the Supervisor and snapped out loudly, "McCullough!" pronouncing my name as if it were a curse.

I was up, front and center, and shakily began: "I think that I shall never see a poem lovely as a tree..." When I finished, I returned to my desk and sat down. The Supervisor came over to my seat and gave me a little holy picture. I said, "Thank you."

I have never, before or since, seen anyone look so confident as Cooper did that day as he walked up to recite. From that day on, whenever I realize that I am feeling as he did that morning, cocksure and calm, I get real nervous.

EXOTIC LUNCH ON A RIVER IN MAINE

Sometimes, a column writes itself. All the writer has to do is just tell what happened. This almost unbelievable 1993 column is an example of that.

I caught up with my friend Ian Baston a couple of weeks ago. He lives outside of Augusta, Maine, in a house he built himself, brick by brick, board by board. I was in Maine to do some white water rafting. I usually get up there a couple of times a year, especially in early May, before the crowds arrive.

I guess I've known Ian for close to ten years. When I first met him, he was a licensed Maine guide, certified to take people down certain rivers in Maine on white water rafting trips. The first river I did with Ian was the Kennebec, one of the largest and historically significant rivers in the state. It rises out of a lake system not far from the Canadian border and empties into the Atlantic a hundred miles later. Over the years, I believe I've done the Kennebec 22 times; Ian's probably done it 200 times.

We had a couple of beers and got to talking about some of the unusual characters we've met over the years we've been doing rafting trips down the Kennebec. Ian worked for Downeast Whitewater, the most professional and highly respected rafting outfit in New England, so he knew his stuff. Working for a company like Downeast also meant that he met a wide variety of people over the years.

When folks come down to Maine for a rafting trip, they tend to come in groups, and those groups tend to be homogeneous. Ten or twelve nurses from Hartford will get together and charter a river trip, or perhaps a bunch of police officers from Boston, lawyers from New Hampshire, or construction workers from Rhode Island.

Almost all of the groups are well-mannered and polite, but every so often, some rowdies will show up at one of the campsites. It was one such group that Ian and I reminisced about while we were talking the other day. It was probably seven or eight years ago. I remember it like it was yesterday. You'll see why in a minute.

We had been on the river for a couple of hours and had stopped to haul the rafts out at a stony beach at a big bend in the river. We flipped the big vessels upside down to empty them of river water, and then flipped them back to dry out in the sun.

Meanwhile, the guides had started a fire on the shore, and produced steak, fish, potatoes, coleslaw and lemonade from a supply boat which had followed us down the river. We had been paddling hard; it felt good to stop for a bit. Although the water temperature was probably in the high 30s, the sun was warm and bright and the first week in May was evident in the alder saplings which lined the river on both sides.

I took off the top to my wetsuit and let the sun beat on my bare shoulders. I got a cup of lemonade and walked along the shore a little, away from the crowd and toward a group of five guys huddled together at the edge of the beach. I found out later that they were from Boston. They looked like city guys; I had noticed them earlier, back at the site where we put into the river earlier that day. They were loud and borderline troublesome. It was obvious that they had been drinking.

They were gathered around a small pile of stuff on the beach: a little mound of material about the volume of three or four softballs. One of the guys tentatively poked it with the toe of his wetsuit bootie. I recognized the material in question immediately. I'd seen plenty of it in the years I've been on the

Maine rivers. The little pile was evidence that a local moose had been able to find food recently and that his digestive system was functioning in a healthy and normal manner. These little brown fiber cannonballs had come out of the rear end of a moose.

One of the guys, a portly man with a neatly-trimmed beard, called over one of the guides and asked him what the stuff was. The guide quickly and correctly identified it. The group laughed long and hard. I remember thinking at the time that there are things in this world which are funny. The little pile of moose droppings on the ground was not one of them.

One of the guys reached down and picked up a small handful of the substance, about the size of a McDonald's plain hamburger on a bun. He held it out for the other guys to see. They looked as if they were beholding a rare and precious stone. In the winter, moose droppings are dry and woody, because of the animals' winter diet. In the spring, the stuff has a little more character to it, being a little more moist and firm.

I stood along the shore, ankle-deep in the swiftly-flowing river, staring at the other shore, but eavesdropping and overhearing the conversation of the quintet a few yards away.

"What's it feel like?" one guy asked.

The man with the handful described what he was feeling.

"What's it smell like?"

He held it close to his nose, and gave his report.

And then a question that definitely had my attention. I turned and looked at them as it was asked.

"I wonder what it tastes like?" the interrogator continued.

They all laughed.

"Twenty bucks." one guy said.

"Twenty bucks what?" the holder of the substance said.

"Twenty bucks if you take a bite out of it, chew it and swallow it."

"No way, Jose."

"Thirty," another guy said.

"Thirty and twenty?" the man holding the moose material said, his voice showing some interest. I couldn't believe what I was hearing.

"Yeah, right," the two friends said. "Fifty bucks."

"OK, you got a deal," the guy said and I then watched him slowly raise the small clump of material to his mouth and take a big bite. His friends let out screams and laughter so loud that the whole campsite turned to look. The man who had just won the bet turned my way to look at the assembly behind me. He had little crumbs of, uh, stuff in his beard as he chewed and swallowed hard, a look on his face like an eight-year-old boy eating his broccoli.

I have since fantasized many times that the man who had the unusual taste experience out on the river that day gets back to Boston and has some stomach trouble as a result of some bacteria or intestinal parasites in his lunch that day.

He goes to the ER and complains about his gastric discomfort. The doctor asks him if he's eaten anything unusual recently.

The man looks around the examining room to see if they are alone, and then turns back and says to the doctor, "Doc, you'd better sit down."

About The Author

Dan McCullough has been travelling and writing since he was a teenager, twice hitchhiking coast-to-coast across America and into Canada and Mexico before he was 20 years old, keeping journals, writing poetry and short stories based on his journeys. Since then he has travelled to Israel, China, Mexico, Central and South America, Egypt, Morocco, the Azores, the Canaries, at least 50 trips to Europe, including every corner of Scotland, all of the major islands of the Caribbean, most of the provinces of Canada, and 47 of the 50 states.

Over the course of his life, he has worked as a dishwasher, golf caddy, bartender, commercial fisherman, landscaper, lobster dealer, sailing instructor, Teamsters' Union trailer-truck driver, technical writer, stonemason, and gravedigger.

As a playwright, his works have seen five productions in southeastern New England. He is the author of dozens of short stories and his work has been printed in several journals. He has published 1,400 newspaper columns and articles in the *Cape Cod Times*, *The Providence Journal*, and other periodicals.

He has been teaching college philosophy for four decades. He did his undergraduate work at Providence College and completed his graduate studies at Boston University. He is currently tenured professor of philosophy at Cape Cod Community College, where he has received the Excellence in Teaching Award.

He has been the resident medical ethicist on the Cape Cod Hospital Ethics Committee for the past 20 years. As a medical ethicist, he has written several articles on medical ethics published in such places as South Africa, Sweden, and Israel. He is the recipient of a Fulbright Grant to study medical ethics in the People's Republic of China.

He is the father of one child, Daniel III, grandfather of two: Alexander and Andrew, and father-in-law to their beloved mother, Kimberly Trudel. He currently resides on Cape Cod, near the fishing village of Rock Harbor, where he has lived most of his life.